BOB HARRINGTON:
God's Happy Hero

Bob going to Washington (Phase I).

BOB
HARRINGTON:
God's Happy Hero

by C. A. Roberts

Publishers since 1798

THOMAS NELSON INC.
NASHVILLE / NEW YORK

Published by Thomas Nelson, Inc., Nashville, Tennessee.
Manufactured in the United States of America

Library of Congress Cataloging in Publication Data
Roberts, Charles A
   Bob Harrington: God's happy hero.
   1. Harrington, Bob, 1927-
BX6495.H267R6   286'.1'0924 [B]   74-4354
ISBN 0-8407-5078-1

Dedication

This book is dedicated
to Bob Harrington's dear friend,
Rex Humbard of Cathedral of Tomorrow,
Akron, Ohio.

Table of Contents

Preface

WHEREAS, deep and abiding faith and reverence, and an intense desire to help his fellow man have always epitomized his efforts; and
WHEREAS, he has coupled his dedication with boundless energy, working endless hours in His cause; and
WHEREAS, he has channeled his efforts into those areas not always reached and sometimes overlooked by others:
NOW, THEREFORE, I Victor H. Schiro, Mayor of the City of New Orleans, do hereby proclaim that Evangelist Bob Harrington be henceforth known as THE CHAPLAIN OF BOURBON STREET and I admonish all citizens to take cognizance thereof, and to offer felicitations to this auspicious occasion.

This book is about the man whom Mayor Schiro proclaimed Chaplain of Bourbon Street: Bob Harrington. This award came to Bob four years after his conversion and eleven years before this writing.

This is not going to be a biography of the life of Bob Harrington. For those interested in such account, I refer you to the book, *The Chaplain of Bourbon Street.**

Rather, this writing will be a year-in-the-life-of Bob Harrington. The time covered in this book will be September, 1972 to December 31, 1973.

* Published by Fleming H Revell.
Company by arrangement with Doubleday & Co. , Inc. 1969

I have chosen this period for several reasons. First, because, during this time, I had the privilege of working closely with Bob. Second, because this was the year when Bob emerged, thanks to television and some events of national importance, as a figure of genuine national prominence. Third, because Bob's story during this time span will prove an inspiration to any person who reads it.

Dr. Jess Moody, Burt Reynolds' minister, tells how Burt won the Rookie of the Year Award in Hollywood, after having been there 13 years. Similarly, the events in this book, which describe an emerging rookie to national television audiences, are the result of fourteen years of hard labor in the school of hard knocks by a man who literally doesn't know the meaning of giving up.

Perhaps a word of explanation should be given about the choice of the title, *Bob Harrington: God's Happy Hero.* The title is obviously brash. But then, Bob is a brash person. Furthermore, Bob sees himself as God's Happy Hero. When asked if he shrinks from this tag, Bob says:

"Not on your life. Young people will get their heroes from somewhere. Who would you rather your son or husband admire and seek to imitate—a no-morals athlete, a nude movie star, or a man who knows who he is, where he is going, and boldly sets out to get there? Jesus Christ is my Superstar, and those who follow me will meet Him."

There is a deeper reason why I would choose the title even if Bob would not for himself. This man's talent lies in his gift with words. He is Will Rogers, Bob Hope, and Don Rickles—with a machine gun delivery dedicated to fostering religious truths. But his true strength is not his gift of gab.

Heroes are supposed to be men of courage, and herein is Bob's strength. A minister is to be known for his faith.

I've never been comfortable with a pat definition for the word, "faith." It has always been easier for me to understand faith from the perspective of a person's actions rather that the propositions which become the objects of faith.

For Bob Harrington, I would define faith as courage: the courage to dare mighty things; the courage not to surrender to obstacles, though seemingly insurmountable.

This book is not fiction, nor does it follow a dramatic plot-line. I hope an interesting story unfolds. I will have failed in my part if a man of courage does not surface in this man of faith, because he is there.

I've always been a believer in heroes. I've had them, cherished them, been inspired by them, and still am. However, this book is not intended to be a subjective praise for one man. I have promised Bob to tell it like it is and hope you will find it that way.

I have been with Bob when he was up, and I have seen him when he was down—way down. I have never seen him walk on water, but I have seen him strike out—not just once, but several times. Those times will be in the book. But they should, because Bob is a home run hitter.

By the time this book reaches print, Henry Aaron will probably have broken Babe Ruth's all time record for home runs. Almost any sports fan knows that Ruth has held the home run record for decades. Few people, however, are aware that he also holds the record for strikeouts. The reason is that the Babe, like most home run hitters, won more times than he lost with his big bat.

Bob is a winner; I believe that or I would not have written this book. Winners sometimes lose just as losers occasionally win. The difference ultimately rests in the attitude of the person involved. A loser rarely knows why he won. He's just glad that he did. But a winner never leaves a loss until he finds out why, corrects himself and tries again.

I'm not really sure that such a commodity exists as "God's Happy Hero," nor even that there should be. But I am convinced that if there are such persons, Bob Harrington is one.

Half way through the year covered in this book, I gave Bob a plaque for his wall. The same plaque hangs in my office. I did not give it to him merely for inspiration, but rather because I felt it applied to him. It is an excerpt from a longer quote from President Theodore Roosevelt:

> *It is far better to dare mighty things, even though checkered by failure, than to take rank with those poor spirits who neither suffer much, nor enjoy much, because they live in that grey twilight that knows neither victory nor defeat.*

The King of Serendip

Bob sat tilted back slightly in his chair, watching the TV
screen against the wall by the door. The chair in which
he was sitting happened to be a barber chair. It looked
just like any other barber chair. In fact, nothing about the
room appeared different from any ordinary barber shop:
mirrors everywhere; outdated magazines; the antiseptic
smell and the plain black phone. Even the television set
fell into the not bad—not good category of most barber
shop TV's. The only possible significance one could bring
to this particular barber shop would be to remind one-
self that it was located just beneath the Oval Office in
the White House.

On the television screen, John Dean was making his
opening statement before the Senate Investigating Committee. The resonant tones of Dean's voice filled the room.
Bob glanced to his left where the head of the FBI for the
White House was sitting and spoke:

"Do you realize this could be one of the most significant
moments in all of history? A man in high office is accusing
the President of wrongdoing, and here we sit not 30 steps
from the President's Office."

One might ask what Bob Harrington was doing in the
White House watching television on the day John Dean

began his famous testimony. The answer is simple: he was there because he is the "King of Serendip."

Most young people sooner or later run into the fairy tale of the King of Serendip who sent his children out to learn the ways of the world. They came upon a camel leader who had lost his camel. The princes set out to help the man find his camel. They did not succeed. However, in the search, they found out that the camel was blind, semi-toothless, lame, and carried honey on one side of his pack and butter on the other side—all this without ever finding the camel. How all this was discovered will be left to a reading of the fairy tale.

From this tale, came a word, "serendipity." In it's simplistic form, serendipity is the art of setting out to find one thing and finding another. Through semantic evolution, the word has achieved much greater sophistication.

A serendipitist is one who accidentally becomes involved in exciting or unusual situations, and yet, although he is accidentally there at the right place, in some inexplicable way, he—the serendipidist—helped plan the accident.

Let's put it another way: unusual things have a way of happening to people who stay on the trail of unusual things. Columbus set out to cross the Atlantic in search of Asia. Instead, he found America. Edison was trying to get an electric light and ended up with a phonograph. Röntgen was trying to improve photography and happened upon a ray he later called "X." Pasteur was trying to find a way to keep his wine from going sour and discovered pasteurization.

In each of the above cases, the man was surprised. However, these were not the kind of surprises that happen to just anyone. They were surprises that occurred to people who were searching night and day for the unusual.

Back to the question as to how Bob Harrington was in Washington, D.C., at the very moment when all America was watching what was happening in the nation's capitol. The simplest and truest answer is that he just happened to be there at the right time. However, it can also be added that the rest of this book could be filled with the names of ministers who didn't happen to be in Washington at this time.

Why Bob? Why this particular time? Was it really an accident, or was it planned? The answer is that it was neither, and yet it was both. Bob was, in fact, in Washington because he was preaching nightly at the ballroom of the Statler Hilton hotel in downtown Washington, D.C.

"Oh," you may respond, "he was in Washington because the head ministerial committee of the combined churches of the Washington area had, one or two years earlier, extended an invitation to Bob to come to Washington."

Not exactly. In fact, not true at all. Bob was there because he had invited himself, not a year earlier, but the previous month. As, in the words of Bob, "God invited me to go to Washington, and I accepted."

Really, it wasn't quite that simple. Or at least there are some other things you should know first that made God invite Bob to go to Washington.

And, by the way, unless my recollection fails me, I have misquoted Bob. As I recall, he actually said, "God ordered me to Washington, and I obeyed." I rejected that particular usage because everyone knows you don't *order* a King; not the King of Serendip. Irrespective of how the request came, to set it in its proper perspective, one must look ten months prior to this occasion: September, 1972.

BOB HARRINGTON:
God's Happy Hero

Bob awaits the start of a crusade service.

CHAPTER I

A Small Step For Many
A Giant Step For Bob
NATIONAL TELEVISION

National television has been an important part of Bob Harrington's ministry. The decision to go this route—a small step for many others—has been a giant step for Bob. It is an important part of his ability to spread the gospel throughout America. Let me share with you the following letter.

August 30, 1972

Mr. George Smith
4739 N. 18th Street
Tampa, Florida 33612

Dear George

It is here! My heart is bursting with joy! The moment you and I have prayed for, dreamed of and worked toward is a reality. Praise the Lord! National TV! This first weekend in September millions of

people are going to see what they have been hearing
about—that It Is Fun Being Saved. And you are a part
of it!

Here is your personal gift—TV Log. We are beginning in 50 cities; in six months, 100 cities: and in one
year, 200 cities. Many of these will be Saturday night
as well as Sunday. You have helped me in the past.
Now I need you to hang in there with me like you
never have before.

First, I need you to help me by making a definite
financial investment in our TV ministry. I am not
sponsored by soap, booze or automobiles. I am supported solely by God and good people like yourself.
Write me today and in return, I will send you a gift
recording of our first TV program.

Second, help me begin a TV "Watch and Pray"
chain for Jesus. Pray for your neighbor; then ask your
neighbor to watch and pray. Pray for your church;
then ask your church to watch and pray. Ask your
unsaved friends and loved ones to watch the TV
show; then pray and watch God's miracle of salvation.

I am counting on your help. Together, through
television, we are going to take Jesus into bars and
brothels, honky tonks and hospitals, prisons and pent-
houses. We have no other choice. We cannot rest
until every lost soul has found rest in Jesus. Send me
your help today, and "Watch and Pray!"

Gratefully saved

Bob Harrington
saved 4-15-58

P.S. You will be blessed by the TV recording—write
soon.

This letter was sent, dated August 30, 1972, to 40,000 names Bob had accumulated from crusades and rallies over the years. He called this list—as many evangelists do—his "mailing list." The implication is that these were his supporters. Each month or so he had been sending these 40,000 names a four page newsletter called *The Heartbeat*. At the time the August 30 letter was sent, Bob did not have the careful mail analysis he would later have. He could not find out, without slowly searching through card boxes, how often he had heard (or how recently) from these original 40,000. He assumed there were 40,000 people out there who believed in Bob Harrington and would be excited about the news of his new television ministry.

On the following Sunday, "Chaplain of Bourbon Street" was shown on 50 television stations across America. The format of the program was in keeping with Bob's ten year ministry along Bourbon Street. Station WWL of New Orleans had a reconstructed nightclub setting complete with bar and runway for the strippers to do their thing.

Of course, real liquor was not in the bottles; nor were the guests at the tables a bona-fide nightclub crowd. But the man doing the preaching had been in hundreds of similar situations in the past ten years where the bullets were real—booze, broads, drunken bums, and all. And he had repeatedly entered these modern day lion's dens of iniquity to proclaim the gospel of Christ in a happy no-holds-barred manner.

The thinking behind this nightclub format for national television was this: it will be a perfect example of being in the world but not of the world. Further, it would be a refreshing alternative to the minister in a long robe behind an austere pulpit. Finally, it would be a subtle reminder that Bob was located in the center of hell and ought to be able to speak about sin with as much authority as any minister in America.

A $50,000 Unsure Thing

Unfortunately enough, most people have some false impressions about the type television venture Bob was entering. There he is before the lights, easily as entertaining, good looking, and magnetic as most television personalities. Either he must be getting paid a handsome fee for his talent, or at least he is being given the time on TV free because he is a minister with a religious program.

And listen to him have the nerve to risk spoiling the spiritual impact by asking the people watching TV to send money.

Bob was not paid to go on television. Nor was he given the time free. In fact, after you read the next few pages, you are going to be driven to one of three conclusions about Bob Harrington: he is a man with (1.) great faith; (2.) no sense; (3.) or a lot of guts.

Beginning with his first week in television, Bob had a minimum new expense of $50,000 per month. Time for each of the fifty stations averaged about $1,000 per month. Cost for producing the four 30 minute programs each month is between five and seven thousand dollars. Making fifty copies of the master tape costs about $10,-000 per month. Therefore, the basic cost for producing and distributing four programs to fifty stations per month —including air time—was often as high as $70,000 per month, but never under $50,000.

Now for Billy, Oral, and Rex, $50,000 per month may be a drop in their bucket. But for Bob, it represented almost twice as much money per month as his ministry had ever brought in. In fact, Bob's budget for his entire ministry was about $50,000 per month when he entered TV. What was he spending $50,000 a month for before he entered television? Office space, chapel and storage room for witnessing materials, books and records on Bourbon Street; a team of associate ministers to help do street preaching and counseling on Bourbon Street.

From the street, all one sees is a door with Bob's name on it. Inside (and upstairs above bars and clubs) Bob has almost a city block of floor space where thousands of visitors come to study, pray in the chapel, and find Christ. At least seventy-five percent of the preparation for Bob's twenty-five crusades per year is handled by his own staff from the Bourbon Street office. Ninety percent of all Bob's books and records are housed, packaged, and shipped from New Orleans. This should give a feel for the way the ministry of Bob Harrington was utilizing a $50,000 per month budget.

Where, then, did he get the money to cover his normal budget? From crusade offerings, book and record sales, rallies, and personal contributions from friends. All this goes directly into the Bob Harrington ministry, which is a non-profit organization.

Bob has no independent income, but rather is on a definite salary from the ministry. And money he receives from any of his speaking engagements—or from any other source—goes to the ministry.

Get this picture in mind: by August of 1972, Bob had a ministry going which was bringing in about $50,000 per month and spending about the same. Bob had worked hard for 10 years to get his ministry in this sound (and solvent) condition.

I can hear some of you saying, "One man spending $50,000 a month!" What you mean is, "He should figure out a way to spend less money and reach more people."

Let me simply inject, at this point, that I could name you dozens of churches with budgets of over a half million dollars (including one I used to pastor) that will not have 200 converts in a year. There will be over 100 nights during the year when 200 people will make decisions for Christ in Bob's meetings (and many other nights when 50 to 100 will come forward).

At this point, I'm not trying to blow Bob's horn. I'm simply stating that if there is such a thing as spending money wisely in religious causes, and if reaching people is a valid criterion for the degree of value, then the money being invested and spent through the Bob Harrington Ministry is money well spent.

Back To Television

Let's get back to television. Agree with me that Bob Harrington, in August, 1972, had a pretty solid thing going. Whether or not you accept his theological motivations, at least accept the fact that every time he received $50, he spent only $49 and a lot of people thought they were being helped by his endeavors.

Get this picture: *next week*—September, 1972, he is going to begin a television ministry that is going to cost him—personally—Bob Harrington—$50,000 *minimum* per month.

Where is he going to get that kind of money? He has no sponsor; he has no church to serve as a "captive buffer"; he has no loan; he has no bond program; no stewardship program; no underwriting of any kind; no "big givers"; no "Board of Directors" (meaning a group of men who, it is understood, will help pay the bills).

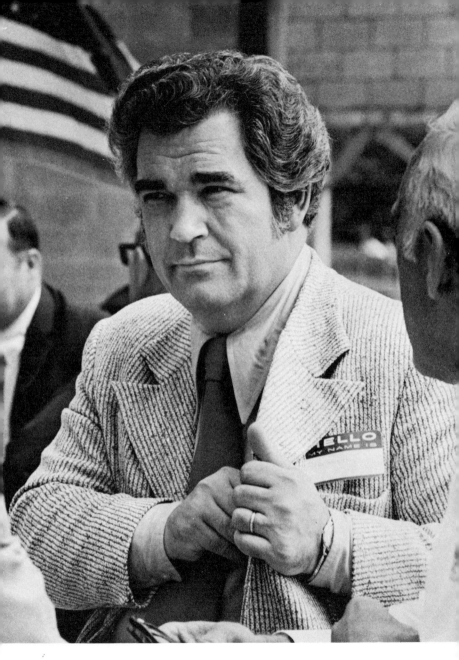

A serious man on the move for Christ.

Bob speaking at the Ohio State Fair.

Bob with his pastor, Dr. J. D. Gray, in front of Bob's church,
The First Baptist Church of New Orleans.

Jack Price directing the crusade choir at Will Rogers Auditorium (Fort Worth Crusade).

Bob with Max Carter (left) who handles distribution of all books and records.

In short, Bob had absolutely no source for that $50,000 per month.

"Ah hah, Bob Harrington is independently wealthy." Sorry, not true. "His wife is wealthy." Wrong again. Joyce is many wonderful things, but wealthy is not one of them.

Where, then, is Bob going to get $50,000 per month? And keep in mind that he has to get it. You don't establish credit with television stations. You pay up or they don't put you on the air next week.

Where is he going to get it? Let's go back to that 40,000 list. All he would need is a dollar and a dime from each of those. The only problem there is that list wasn't any good, and Bob knew it. A mailing list is a funny thing; you feed it—mail to it—or it dies. During a ten year period, that 40,000 would go months—and sometimes years—without hearing from Bob. And Bob had gone years without hearing from many of them.

In short, until he entered television, Bob had never done much about handling his mail properly. I know because I, as president of Church Systems Computer Company, took over Bob's mail program at the same time he entered television.

One of the first things I did was ask Ron Sowers, Bob's business manager, what kind of response they had received from the last mailing to that 40,000. He said, 300; less than 1%. Most of the successful donor ministries get between 8 and 15% response. Below 3%, you are losing money with every mailing.

So we had a suspicion from the beginning that the 40,000 list was poor. (Our suspicions were later confirmed. After four months of mailing about Bob's television, 38,967 of the original 40,000 never even responded once!)

Bob on the streets of Jerusalem—the French Quarter of New Orleans.

Where, then, was Bob going to get this new $50,000 per month? Simple, you might suggest. People who watch television will give the money.

That is ultimately true. But please note the word *ultimate*. The normal time period for bringing a station to the place where the people in the area will pay for it —or that a station will pay for itself—is one year. Rex Humbard recently said that it can easily take two full years for a TV station to pay for itself.

And please understand what is meant by "pay for itself." This means that after X amount of months (or years), a station is bringing in, in a given month, as much as it cost for the TV time for the month.

This means the *future* looks bright. But what about the past? It also means that for X number of months (or years) one has been going in the hole. When he finally breaks even, he may be breaking even bankrupt!

Look at it this way. Rex Humbard, the King of Television, (no one ever is on more stations at one time except when the President is trying to explain something) says one year is a good pay out time.

So, on this basis, Bob spends $50,000 the first month and gets back $5,000. The second month he spends $50,-000 and gets $10,000; the third month, he spends $50,000 and gets $15,000; and the fourth month—$50,000 and $20,000.

Total: After four months, he has spent $200,000. And this is true only if he does better than average. In short, if Bob Harrington does *better* than Rex Humbard, Billy Graham, and Oral Roberts, he will only be $150,000 in the hole after four months!

These are the odds Bob was facing when he made the decision to go into national television.

And Bob said, "We'll get it; let's go."

Now that either is an act of stupidity or poor judgment. Why would a grown man fight the odds to such a fantastic degree as this?

In Person He Is Different

Against outlandish odds Bob said, "Let's go!" Why? Because Bob Harrington thinks he is different! Different from Rex Humbard; different from Oral Roberts; different from Billy Graham.

He thinks he is able to outdraw any of these men when given an equal chance.

On the surface, this sounds like a super-ego that has lost all sense of proportion. But let's examine the matter more closely.

Bob Harrington has more crowd appeal than any evangelist in America, including Billy Graham. You put Rex Humbard, Oral Roberts, Billy Graham, and Bob Harrington in auditoriums, side by side, with the same opening night crowd, and no other preparation other than their own appeal, and Bob Harrington will leave all three of these in a cloud of dust. First, he is funnier than any of them, and Americans like to be entertained; second, he would have each of them without their crutch: Billy with his "I am religion for America" image; Rex with his 300 stations, and Oral without the implication that he still heals blindness and cancer when we all know he has long since gone on to better things.

Bob Harrington is the drawing-power-personality among religious circles today. Billy Graham people start a year in advance and spend $250,000 per crusade. (So says Executive Director George Wilson.) And they lose money in every crusade. The reason is that they—the

Billy Graham people—will spend any amount of money to keep Billy from ever being caught preaching to an empty seat. God forbid! Rex Humbard has resigned himself to preach to less people in person. He is preaching to fewer in person than before, because he is spending less money than before.

I really don't know what Oral is doing other than telling people that something good is going to happen to them. I think he gave up personal appearances after his last healing service—except for Johnny Carson and Oral Roberts University basketball games.

In 1972, Bob Harrington started a week in Cobo Hall in Detroit with 2,000 people. He had practically no precrusade preparation. He finished the week with 10,000 in Cobo Hall.

In 1972, Bob began in San Antonio's Convention Center with 2,000. He finished with 10,000.

Rex Humbard has had Bob two weeks a year for the past five years (Memorial week and Thanksgiving week). Why? Because Bob draws people like no other preacher in America!

Why Not TV?

Bob Harrington draws a crowd in person. Recently a midwestern evangelist, Lowell Lundstrom, was explaining why he invited Bob to Sisseton, South Dakota.

He said, "The people up here love me. During the past 14 years the largest crowd I have been able to draw of my own people in my own territory was 3,500. I invited Bob to preach my anniversary, and the crowd jumped to 5,500 with no additional expense.

So, Bob's reasoning was this; if he could outdraw any preacher in America in person, if given an equal chance, why shouldn't he be able to outdraw them on television?

Bob's Goal For The Seventies

This was certainly not Bob's only motivation, although it was a central factor in giving him courage to try. Bob, in the summer of 1972, set forth a goal which, he is convinced, was given to him by God: *that, in the Seventies, in America; every eye shall see, and every ear hear; and every heart feel, that It's Fun Being Saved!*

Bob has a thing about America. He thinks God has called him to wake it up *in this decade!* I have tried, without success to interest him in Europe, or the Far East. However, at this writing, he is seriously working out a plan to try to preach to all of America, in person in one year! (To be discussed later) In recent years, he has been preaching twenty-five crusades per year. (Billy Graham has never preached more than twelve crusades in one year.)

Bob's reasoning is this: either he must admit that the "Every eye—every ear" phrase is empty nonsense, or he must be willing to take advantage of every means toward reaching this end.

And "Every eye—every ear" means television—at least if it is to happen in the seventies—or even this century!

Look at the numbers: Bob's normal "peak crowd" in a crusade is 10,000 a night.

Let's say that in 25 crusades he reached this crowd every night of a crusade. That would mean eight nights × 10,000 people × 25 weeks. That would be 2 million people in one year. Not bad. But facing a population of above 200,000,000 in America, Bob would reach his "Every eye—every ear" goal—not in the 1970's but 100 years later in the 2,070's!

Now add TV. With 30 of the right TV stations—not 50—30—Bob's TV audience is six million per week! It doesn't take Einstein to do some quick figuring and come out with 312 million in one year.

Sure, it is not six million different people each week. But remember this: if he can whip the quantity problem in *one* year instead of 100, he has seven more years in the seventies to add and subtract stations—go to prime time—anything—to up-grade the quality of the viewing audience until, in the 70's, every eye has seen and every ear heard and every heart felt that's It's Fun Being Saved!

O.K., O.K. This all sounds good. But its August, 1972. Bob is already using up his revenue to keep his ministry going. He is going to add TV stations in September to the tune of $50,000 minimum!

The odds of one of those 50 stations paying for itself from the start are 50 to 1; of half of them paying from the start, 5,000 to 1; of all of them paying from the start, 500,000 to 1!

Every major minister I know—and I know them all—who entered TV in the past 20 years, did so with some kind of ace in the hole—either a church, or a loan, or a group of money men, or a tested and true mailing list. And I'm talking about all the ones you have heard of and many you haven't heard of.

But, Bob Harrington, Chaplain of Bourbon Street, in September of 1972, was breaking the mold. He was going against the odds when the odds were 100% against him.

And, in all candor, I must tell you he never batted an eye. I sat in his study in August of 1972. I had mixed emotions; like your mother-in-law going over the cliff in your new Cadillac. Bob was about to become the biggest single account for my computer company. But deep inside I felt I was about to launch my ship by sinking his.

This was our conversation on August 6, 1972 in Bob's office in New Orleans: I spoke;

"Bob, I honestly don't think you will be able to keep TV money coming in fast enough to keep from going under."

His response didn't come with the flowery alliterations that mark his public delivery. There was neither joy nor optimism in his response, only a sense of purpose that emerged from a sober continence.

"C.A., if I don't try to reach America in the 70's, I'll spend my last years in an old folks home asking myself why I didn't. The way I'm going now, (with his 50 TV stations plan) my *only* problem will be money. I know we can reach the people. I know they need Christ, I know many will respond.

"And, if all that happens, I would rather stay awake at night wondering how to pay for what God wanted me to do—reach America—rather than stay awake at night wondering why I didn't do what God wanted me to do."

"Jesus would never have given us the great commission to *go tell our world* if He had known for sure there would be no way to finance it."

I sat there with a cold feeling running through me; not a good feeling at all, for I knew that there literally was not going to be an easy answer to the problem Bob was creating for himself.

And yet, something good was mixed in my emotions— and probably I shouldn't mention it here—but I think it integral to Bob's story.

For 15 years of my life, I gave myself to a complete commitment to Jesus Christ and the ministry. I lived under the conviction that God could do anything but fail.

Then, for reasons unimportant to the readers who do not know me, I lost this grip of faith and courage on life, the ministry, and myself. I could remember the day when I would fly to Brazil and return to raise $150,000 in six weeks for 26 churches and 26 preachers in Brazil.

But that light went out for me. And for five long years I had no reason for wanting to enter the fight again.

My faith had been shaken; and my desire; and my love for God! And religious talk bored me, when it didn't repel me.

But on that August day in 1972, I sat before a very talented man who had the guts to lay it all on the line. And down inside of me some spark rekindled.

We picked up the phone and made the call. On the following Sunday, Bob Harrington, Chaplain of Bourbon Street would become a national figure on 50 TV stations across America at a minimum cost of $50,000 per month.

And the one truly important question was the only one we studiously avoided on that August day in New Orleans in 1972. Where is the money coming from?

CHAPTER II

Operation a Success
Patient Almost Dead
TV RESPONSE

The fall of 1972 may well have been, for Bob, the happiest time in his ministry to that point. He had been riding a high anticipation of launching his national television program, "Chaplain of Bourbon Street." It had been his dream, conception and prayer, and he had done it his way.

In the past twenty years, many aspiring ministers had hit the TV trail. Most of them followed a similar pattern: find a good station; get it on its feet; then add a second; then a third.

Bob chose to let it all hang out with one roll of the camera. Actually, he did not start completely from scratch. For ten years, he had been preaching ever expanding crusades. He rarely, on any night, spoke to fewer than 3,000.

He was also not a new face to television. He had been on national talk shows throughout the country for years. He had also preached several times to the national TV audiences afforded by appearances with Rex Humbard at the Cathedral of Tomorrow.

It will probably not be necessary to the reader to be

introduced to Rex Humbard. This minister from Akron, Ohio, has preached to more men than any minister in all of history—including Billy Graham. Every week he is seen on over 300 TV stations around the world. His one hour service is seen each week by over 22 million people.

Rex Humbard is an intelligent, down to earth, dedicated man. He and Bob have almost a David and Jonathan friendship. When many other preachers have chosen to give Bob the benifit of the dirt, Rex has chosen to love him, admire his talent and truly be his friend.

Bob has returned this respect and admiration in full measure. Every year for the past five years, Bob has spoken at Cathedral of Tomorrow Memorial Day Week and Thanksgiving Week. Rex says Bob is the only preacher who can draw a crowd to the 5,000 seat Cathedral on these holiday weeks. This one relationship gave Bob a decided edge both in his crusade attendance, and his own entrance to national television.

The mail response to "Chaplain of Bourbon Street" was strong from the outset. It was evident that many were being reached by Bob's media message.

He did not experience an early response financially. Bob had a lot to learn about cultivating money support through the mail. He began by offering a long playing record to anyone who would send a contribution. This meant a person could send in a dollar and get a five dollar record. Unfortunately, since most of us are motivated by a "what's in it for me" philosophy, most people have a way of gravitating toward avenues where they can get the most for the least.

Vaughn Mancha, one time Athlete Director at Florida State University, used to say: "It matters not if you win or lose, or even how you play the game, but what is the take at the gate." Bob's "take at the gate" on TV was completely out of proportion to his large mail response from the beginning in September, 1972.

Based on the facts in the previous chapter, this should lead to the conclusion that Bob was in trouble financially from the start of his TV venture. This was not the case for several reasons. Bob's ministry was in good financial condition when he entered TV. He had saved every penny he could to give TV a chance to get off the ground.

Bob had also geared his own activities, in the fall of 1972, to feed TV. He added to the number of crusades he had scheduled. He filled his normally free time between crusades with one night rallies where he took offerings for TV.

Ironically, one of the biggest factors working against Bob was his faith in himself and the fact that God would see him through. This became a negative factor to the extent that Bob's success image made it difficult for people to believe that he really needed their help.

Another negative factor Bob has had to contend with is his ministerial life-style which has always had a way of both isolating as well as attracting people. He never pastored a church. Most of his sermons for the first ten years of his ministry were preached in bars, strip joints and nightclubs. His converts were usually club owners, strippers, bartenders and bums. There is an extremely large circle of Christendom that feels neither Bob, nor Jesus for that matter, should entertain such an offbeat ministry.

Also, Bob has never been able, or at least willing to adapt his pace and temperament to others. He decided long ago that he could not reach America in the Seventies if he waited on local Christians to invite him to their city. When he feels led to go to a certain city, he picks up the phone and rents the civic center. Most preachers sub-

Bob signing autographs after speaking at the Ohio State Fair.

Bob with Miss Texas who sang and played for one of Bob's January television programs. She attended almost every night of the Fort Worth Crusade.

scribe to a territorial imperative philosophy. They somehow feel the territory where they minister is theirs to
control. They don't want an evangelist entering their
territory until he is invited. They then want him to take
out only a modest amount of money—the sum to be determined by them—and certainly he—the evangelist—is
not entitled to the names and addresses of the people in
their territory. From Bob's perspective, America is his
territory. Therefore, he often comes in uninvited, receives
a generous offering and leaves with names and addresses
that he adds to his own mailing list. This approach has
been one of Bob's strengths. It has also cost him a lot
of church and preacher support. (This will be discussed
more fully in a later chapter.)

Most evangelists have also made good use of a board
of directors and a secondary board of advisors. The idea
is to have periodic meetings with these key men. Let
them help plan future endeavors and make key decisions
regarding financial expenditures. Since most of these men
were selected primarily for their personal financial
strength, the more they become involved in directing
the ministry, the more of their financial strength they will
lend.

Bob has a board of directors, but not of the ordinary
sort. Bob keeps these men informed regarding every aspect
of the ministry. Some of them couldn't buy their way out
of a paper bag. He uses these men to help him see that the
Bob Harrington Ministry conforms to all the regulations
of a sound non-profit organization.

But no one directs Bob's ministry but Bob. When he is
convinced that a certain thing should be done, that becomes a majority. In theory, this approach is no different
from Billy Graham's. It's just that Bob has the advantage
—like Graham—of being his own man, but also the disad-

vantage of not having had the enormous public head start of Graham.

The above information is integral to an understanding of what happened to Bob in the late Fall of 1972. By November, Bob had tapped his crusades to the limit. December and January are not strong crusade months for any evangelist. His ministry's financial reserves were expended. Mailing costs were rising. An evangelist has to invest in two mailings before he begins to get returns from the first. If he is doing something wrong in his mail, four months can go by before results begin to come from a new approach. If the second approach is also fruitless, he will be out of business before he can recover.

Bob initiated two major programs in late November and December: one regarding the effort to get big gifts personally and one regarding a Christmas mailing. Both brought too little and too late.

Keep in mind that Bob's whole attitude was positive and happy in mid-November of 1972. He was getting sounds of approval regarding his TV ministry from every corner of the United States. His crusade crowds were swelling, a by-product of TV exposure.

In fact, Bob was feeling so good that he bought a set of golf clubs and brought them to Houston where he was speaking for the weekend. Since I live on a golf course south of Houston, Quail Valley Golf Club, Bob joined me at 7:30 on Saturday morning for a game of golf. After six holes, Bob decided there were more important things to do and we returned to the coffee shop. Sitting there with Jack Price and myself, Bob began to discuss his burden for the financial needs of his TV ministry.

He took a napkin and began to draw off a brochure for a special Christmas mailing that would offer a package of books and records. At this point we did not yet know that the greater part of his 40,000 mailing list was worthless. Bob suggested that we also rent a list of a religious periodical that he appeared in regularly. The list contained 50,000 names. It sounded like a good idea to me, which shows how young and inexperienced I was in the mailing business. You don't just send an expensive mailing to a completely new list. You send a test mailing of a few thousand.

But not us. By the time breakfast was over, we had the special mailing laid out. It was going to include an appeal for help with TV. Just think—50,000 new supporters! This would mean Bob now had almost 100,000 people to mail to. I cringe when I reflect on this stupid number trap that sane men can fall into. We figured that if 1200 people responded, the mailing would be paid for. Anything above that would be profit for TV. I will spare you the results for a few paragraphs.

Bob's schedule for December was fairly free. He decided that the only thing that would save the TV ministry would be to get some big money men to give some big money.

Let me explain, at this point, why I am using the caption, we. I was still president of Church Systems. Bob was my biggest account. In fact, he was 80% of my company's revenue. I not only helped with his mail, but also printed his *Heartbeat* newsletter. But Bob was more than an account to me. I had become emotionally involved in what he was trying to do. As the odds grew more and more against his succeeding, I became more determined to help him succeed.

We went to work on a flip chart that would give a man, or a small group of men, an idea of Bob's goals and needs. In rough form, it went something like this:

(1.)

WHY SHOULD YOU
INVEST IN
THE BOB HARRINGTON MINISTRY?

(2.)

BOB HARRINGTON
HAS A GOAL
TO REACH AMERICA
IN THE SEVENTIES

(3.)

BOB HARRINGTON'S
GOAL
IS CLEARLY DEFINED

* EVERY MAN—WOMAN AND YOUNG PERSON

IN

* EVERY HOME IN

* EVERY CITY IN AMERICA

(4.)

EVERY EYE SHALL SEE

EVERY EAR SHALL HEAR

EVERY HEART CAN FEEL

THAT

IT'S FUN BEING SAVED

(5.)

BOB HARRINGTON HAS A PLAN

FOR ACHEIVING HIS GOAL

TO MARSHALL THE STRENGTH

OF EVERY MEDIA

THAT REACHES PEOPLE IN AMERICA

(6.)

BOB HARRINGTON'S PLAN

PROJECTED INTO 73

* A MAJOR METROPOLITAN CRUSADE EACH

MONTH

* 50 NEW TV STATIONS EVERY 4 MONTHS

* NIGHTLY RALLIES FROM COAST TO COAST

* A PERSONAL DAILY RESPONSE TO ALL WHO

  WRITE FOR HELP

(7.)

BOB HARRINGTON

HAS A METHOD

MEN

PREACH TO	MEN
REACH	MEN
WIN	MEN
TRAIN	MEN
TO WITNESS TO	MEN

GOD'S METHOD IS *MEN*

(8.)

BOB HARRINGTON

HAS A MOTIVE

TO BUILD SOULWINNERS

NOT A	*BUT A*
BANK	WITNESSING BANKER
CHURCH	WITNESSING MINISTER
SCHOOL	WITNESSING PRINCIPAL
BUSINESS	WITNESSING BUSINESSMAN

(9.)

HOW CAN YOU HELP?

(10.)

THE SPIRIT AND THRUST OF

BOB HARRINGTON'S MINISTRY

IS U R G E N C Y !

(11.)

THE ONLY THING

BOB HARRINGTON

CANNOT *BUY*

WITHOUT LARGE

ADDITIONAL HELP

IS

T I M E ! !

(12.)

THE GENEROUS CONTRIBUTIONS

OF

ONE DEDICATED CHRISTIAN MAN

COULD SPELL

THE DIFFERENCE IN

76   and   75

74   and   73

REGARDING AMERICA'S SPIRITUAL DESTINY

(13.)

TV DOES TWO THINGS

* MAKES BOB HARRINGTON A HOUSEHOLD WORD

* LET'S BOB HARRINGTON BEGIN RESHAPING AMERICA'S MORALS

WHERE IT SHOULD BEGIN

IN THE HOME

(14.)

* THE GROWTH OF

    THE BOB HARRINGTON MINISTRY

* THE GROWTH OF

    CRUSADES

* THE GROWTH OF

    BOB'S SOULWINNING ARMY

* THE GROWTH OF

    A NEW AMERICA FOR CHRIST

        IS ALL RELATED TO

* THE GROWTH OF

    THE TV MINISTRY

(15.)

$1,000 PER MONTH OR $12,000 WILL

UNDERWRITE

ONE NEW TV STATION FOR ONE YEAR

$1,000 PER MONTH REACHES

120,000 PEOPLE PER MONTH!

(16.)

BOB HARRINGTON'S MINISTRY HAS COME

THIS FAR WITH THE HELP OF

B U D D I E S

NOW HE NEEDS

B I G   B U D D I E S

LIKE YOURSELF

(17.)

AMERICA ABOVE ALL ELSE—IS SEEKING

HAPPINESS

BOB HARRINGTON HAS A MESSAGE—IT'S

BEING SAVED

YOU—CAN BRING THE TWO TOGETHER

(18.)

BECOME BROTHER BOB'S

B I G   B U D D Y

AMERICA'S MEN   ARE WAITING

AMERICA'S YOUNG

PEOPLE   ARE WAITING

AMERICA'S HOMES   ARE WAITING

WE MUST HURRY !

(19.)

WILL YOU HELP?

WANTED!

MEN WHO WILL JOIN

BOB HARRINGTON'S

BIG BUDDY 1000 CLUB

* 1,000 MEN WHO WILL GIVE $100 PER MONTH

* 100 MEN WHO WILL GIVE $1000 PER MONTH

WILL YOU BECOME A

B I G   B U D D Y

We spent December giving presentations to groups and waiting for the results of the regular December mailing and the special Christmas mailing.

As far as the presentations, they were a total bust. Men just don't let go of money for things they are not involved in to some degree. Bob has some men who support his ministry, but most of them were saved in one of his crusades.

The mailings were a disaster. It was at this point that we were able to purge Bob's original list to get the results of four months of passionate appeal to support the TV ministry. It was here that we found only 1,400 people on that list who were helping Bob. The 50,000 special list drew 85 responses.

The new year was one week old and Bob was $150,000 in debt. If he got out of TV immediately and was very careful, he could get out of debt by the end of 1973.

Bob went to the bank. The banker agreed to lend Bob $100,000 if he would put up all the assets of his ministry as collateral including the house in which he and his family lived.

It was at this point that Joyce, Bob's wife, put her foot down. Their house, although it was owned by the ministry, was paid for. And it represented the one piece of security the Bob Harrington family had ever known.

Joyce had lived by faith in God and Bob. Bob had lived by faith alone. This sounds a little trite, but it is a fact. Recently, Bob had a conversation with Fred Swank, who has been pastor of Sagamore Hill Baptist Church for about 40 years. Dr. Swank made this remark; "I have never had to live by faith. I have always had a house and a car and a salary provided for me."

Bob has always been his own employer. He has always paid himself. Many times he has had to skip giving himself a pay check.

It was a great day for the Harrington household when they burned the note on their home. They had a place to call their own. It was a testimony to the diligent efforts by Bob to care for his family.

Now the house was about to become tied to a debt far greater than the value of the house. A woman's security—even though her faith be in God, as with Joyce—her security is in her man and her home.

It wasn't fair to Joyce and Mitzi and Rhonda, the two daughters who were students at Baylor. There had to be another way.

But there wasn't. It was a mortgage on the ministry and the home, or TV was dead. Bob signed the papers and left for Miami to preach his famous sermon, "It's Fun Being Saved."

The baby, called national television, had been born and was, for the present, safely snuggled in an incubator. Bob's problem was to keep oxygen and heat in the incubator long enough to let the child get by on its own. In the days to come, Bob was determined to go at his job harder than ever before. But there are only so many days and nights and Bob had been giving them all. What new thing he could do was, as yet, undiscovered.

CHAPTER III

A Women's Place
A Man's Experience

When I first discussed with Bob the subject of serving as a consultant to his ministry, the two of us were standing late at night in a Holiday Inn parking lot. I vividly remember his remarks:

"C. A., whatever happens, I'm not ever going to beg people to help me win people to Christ. If it ever comes to that, I want you to take a picture of me down on my knees with my hands clasped before me and the word PLEASE in bold print beneath the picture. Then after you take the picture, shoot me and throw the picture away."

The idea of pleading with Christians to spend a few dollars to help win souls seemed to Bob not only sinful in some way, but plain unmanly. In ten years he had never begged, and he had always found a way to keep going. In fact, Bob told me he made a practice of paying bills by return mail. It had not been easy through the years for him to build a ministry with office space, storage space, counselling areas, staff—demanding over a half million dollars a year—and yet bring it to a place where the ministry was absolutely solvent—with money in the bank. But he had done it.

What Bob was going through in January of 1973 was a new experience.

It was a terrible disappointment to him to have to face the facts about the poor mail response and the even poorer response from groups to make large gifts for the TV ministry. He took it all as some kind of personal failure on his part.

It was brought to his attention that those 1400 "good ones" on his list had given more than one should ever dream possible. And he was definitely picking up new support each month from crusades and TV. However, none of this changed the plain truth that he was in a race against time with the odds ever increasingly against him.

True, the $100,000 loan had temporarily brought him even with the world (including another $50,000 by a company that was very interested in and sympathetic toward Bob.) He was back where he had been in September with certain exceptions: (1.) he had a new $5,000 per month principal and interest payment (2.) he had a far more realistic appraisal of what he could count on from his active supporters. (3.) he knew now that the mere act of showing up on TV was not going to bring floods of financial support from viewers.

Upon reflection, I cannot recall Bob showing, to me, one sign of hesitancy or doubt that January. To quote Bob about himself, "He is a strange person." He can mask his feelings as well as any man I ever met. In the pulpit, he plays every human emotion like a violin. But in person he maintains a steadiness that always borders on the positive.

At the January, 1973 stage of our relationship, I had only known Bob for 5 months, and I did not know him well at that time. A few months later, he would be closer to me than a brother. But that January, I was struggling, trying to build my own computer company while Bob was trying to save his ministry. I worked with about 20 other churches and 20 other ministries throughout the nation and had plenty else to do than bear Bob's problems. Besides, I couldn't afford to think things were really bad for Bob because I needed his business for my company. I think Bob sensed that and for that reason did not share too much of himself at that stage in our relationship.

In January of 1973, Bob was carrying about all the burden one man should have to carry at one time. TV was struggling for survival. Like a tiger by the tail, there did not seem, to Bob, any way to let go without admitting failure. He was in debt, mortgaged to the hilt. His family evidenced, for the first time, that Bob might not be doing the right thing, for himself, for his family and maybe even for God.

But Bob was going to make it. He started the new year like a whirlwind: Galveston, Texas January 5–7; New Orleans for TV taping January 9–12; Clewiston, Florida January 13; Fort Meyers, Florida January 15–22; Birmingham, Alabama January 23; Miami, Florida January 26–28. Everywhere he went he preached like a dying man. He called men to repentance and always he closed by making a plea for help with his TV ministry.

How his health remains, only God knows. In each of the above cities, you can count on Bob preaching at night. But you must also figure at least two schools and two radio and TV programs per day, plus at least one civic club. He is never in bed before midnight and he is always up by 7 AM.

Joyce came to be with Bob while he was in Miami. She had planned to stay the weekend but something happened to alter her plans.

The two of them were driving to the motel after the evening service. Bob was driving, thinking how good it was to have Joyce with him. He never liked to be alone

when he was so tired. And he could always count on
Joyce to boost his spirits, especially now that she knew
the pressure he was under. When Joyce spoke, it was not
exactly what Bob expected to hear.

"Bob, do you ever read your Bible, or pray anymore?"

Bob swung a glance in her direction then looked ahead
again.

"What do you mean by that?"

"I mean," she continued, "that you used to spend so
much time around the room reading your Bible and praying. You used to wake me up in the morning to show me
a verse. I used to hear you turn on the light by your side
of the bed. You would be on your knees in the middle of
the night. Lately, all you do is stay on the telephone:
TV, TV, mail, mail, *Heartbeat, Heartbeat,* business, business. And then you fall into bed exhausted. You don't
even say goodnight to me lately, much less God."

She should have stopped there. Who knows, she may
have won her point right on the spot. We will never know,
for like a loving, caring, companion, she bore in for the
kill.

"I really wonder how you can stand up there night after
night and tell people to pray and read their Bibles, if you
aren't going to do it yourself."

"Well, my girl, you won't have to worry about watching me, because I'm going to remove this poor example
from you for the rest of the weekend."

"Now, Bob, you can't get mad at me for telling the
truth. And I wouldn't say anything about it if I were not
deeply concerned."

There was no more talk in the car. When they reached
the room, Bob called National Airlines and made a reser-
vation for one on the first plane out, which left at 8:15
AM. He then undressed, turned out the light and went to
sleep without saying goodnight—to God or Joyce.

He was still asleep at 6:00 the next morning when Joyce awoke, dressed and left for the airport, alone.

Joyce Harrington is an unusual woman. She has the grace and charm that is the usual stock in trade for most genuine southern women. You get the feeling when she talks to you that she is just thrilled to be talking with you. You must not get discouraged if you hear her showing the same exuberance when talking with the garbage man. This is a southern woman. She is gracious by nature and at all times.

Joyce is a dedicated Christian. At this writing, she is the Director for the Woman's Missionary Union for her church, the First Baptist Church of New Orleans.

She is also a very intelligent woman. She serves actively as a corporate officer in Bob's ministry. She can perform almost any job necessary at the office, and often does.

Most of all, Joyce knows Bob. She has been there for it all. She loves him, believes in him, and is his number one fan.

Joyce's only shortcoming that I know of is that she is a woman. And women refuse to learn that you do not confront a super-ego. You try infiltration or some sort of subtlety. But not direct assault. She could have left an apple on the open Bible; or knelt herself by the bed in prayer (no, that would definitely not work.)

But she said it. Later, her only defense was that she had been thinking it for over a month and only said it, when she could no longer be silent. At any rate, she said it, and—sad or glad—flew into the morning for New Orleans.

The next week Bob and Joyce were supposed to go to the National Religious Broadcasters Convention in Washington, D.C. They were to be at the head table where Bob was to appear on the program with Pat Boone, Stephen Alford, and Billy Graham. They had made plans to

Jack Price singing (Fort Worth Crusade).

Bob signing autographs for his fans.

One of Bob's "Buddies" helps promote his television program.

A rolling advertisement for the crusade.

go to Washington from Miami. Bob went to Washington alone.

When he arrived at the Washington Hilton, there was a note to call Mrs. Harrington in New Orleans. He didn't return the call.

An hour later, the phone rang in Bob's room. It was Joyce. She asked if she was still coming to Washington with him. He said she wasn't. (All women get ready to fall in love with this girl.)

Joyce informed Bob that she was coming anyway; that she had seen the invitation, and it definitely said Reverend and Mrs. Harrington. She hung up the phone. Six hours later she was sitting before the mirror in Bob's room getting ready for the NRB banquet.

Whoever made the placements put Bob and Joyce at opposite ends of the head table. Pat Boone spoke first. Then Bob said a few words. Billy Graham followed for about five minutes referring to Bob as God's whirlwind. Each of these three had been brief because the main speaker was Dr. Stephen Alford, Minister of The Calvary Baptist Church in Manhattan, New York.

He spoke from the text, "Not by might, nor by power, but by my Spirit, saith the Lord." He talked about ministers who try to do everything with their own might instead of God's might. He spoke of ministers who try to do it all in the flesh, because they, in fact, want the glory to come to them. He talked about ministers who were too busy serving God to find time to pray and read their Bibles. He said such men were laboring in the flesh and not the Spirit and ultimately their labors would be in vain and for nothing.

As Dr. Alford spoke, a man and a woman wept openly at opposite ends of the head table. When Dr. Alford finished, Bob got out of his seat and walked past Pat Boone,

Billy Graham, and Dr. Alford. He took Joyce in his arms before the crowd and weeping, whispered in her ear: "I'm going to read my Bible; and I'm going to pray; and I'm going to be a better husband, and a new man."

The next week, the people on Bob's mailing list received this letter:

February, 1973

Miss Joann Howard
7413 Evans Avenue
Jackson Mississippi 39200

DEAR Joann

PLEASE DON'T PUT THIS DOWN! Something has happened that I want to share with you. This is a new Bob Harrington writing you. Last week I sat in Washington and listened while another man preached on the Scripture, "Not by might nor power, but my Spirit, saith the Lord." And God spoke to my heart.

"Bob," He said, "Too much your might and not enough My Spirit." And I had to say, "Guilty, Lord." So I wanted you to know that God works on preachers, too. I wanted you to know I have rededicated this ministry to the leadership of the Spirit. And I want to tell you in all honesty what happened to me in the last few months.

As you know, we began our TV ministry this last fall. As sure as I am here, God led in that decision. I wish you could see the response we are getting concerning people being saved all over the nation. I have preached to more people in the past five months through TV than all the other years of my ministry.

Now, please, let me, in a spirit of love, tell it like it is. I asked many of you to help share the financial load of this great soul winning endeavor. And many of you have. But many did not. I guess at that point, I trusted more in men and myself than the Lord.

So I kept going longer and harder, pushing my health to the straining point. All that is over. Our TV ministry is going on. And I am going too, but trusting completely in the Spirit of God to direct and supply. I ask you to join me in prayer for this matter. And if the Spirit of God leads you, I ask you to help. I know God will lead enough of you to see us through.

Gratefully saved

Bob Harrington

P.S. When you write, ask for a free copy of "The Chaplain of Bourbon Street"

Bob called his staff together and shared the experience with them. He called me and told me about it. There was no question that Bob had truly been moved deeply.

During the next few weeks, he spent every spare moment pouring through his Bible. During this time, Bob worked out what he called an open analysis of himself before God. It was later printed in the *Heartbeat*. It reminds one of a passage from the confessions of Augustine. The following is Bob's confession, which he called: "Daily De-selfing."

Daily De-selfing

"What does this mean? Why is it needed? Who needs to do it? How is it done and when? These are some of the questions I will touch on in this mini-message which could give maxi-results.

"The condition of God's blessing is absolute surrender of all into His hands. Praise God! If our hearts are willing for that, there is no end to what God will do for us, and to the blessing God will bestow.

I have begun to make it my daily prayer; Lord, teach me absolute surrender. In my travels I preach in churches over America . . . major city-wide crusades and I have come to believe the greatest need of the believer and the church is "absolute surrender". Are you willing to surrender yourself absolutely into His hands? Could this be your problem?

"The Temple of Solomon was absolutely surrendered to God when it was dedicated to Him. And every one of us is a temple of God, in which God will dwell and work mighty on one condition—absolute surrender to Him. 'It is God that worketh in us, both to will and to do of his good pleasure.' God Himself will come in to turn out what is wrong, to conquer what is evil and to work what is well-pleasing in His blessed sight God Himself will work it in you. He will have to because I am not able. I pray you learn to know and trust God now. Say this as I do daily: "Lord, I am willing that you should make me willing."

"Christ Jesus: He lived a life of absolute surrender and He has possession of you and me (the saved). He is living in mine and your saved heart by His Holy Spirit."

"To whom God would make known what is the riches of the glory of this mystery among the gentiles; which is Christ in you, the hope of glory."

Colossians 1:27

"It's my prayer for you, be occupied with God. We want to get help, every one of us, so that in our daily life God shall be cleared to us, God shall have the right place, and be 'all in all'. If God allows the sun to shine upon you moment by moment, without intermission, will not God let His life shine upon you every moment? And why have you not experienced it? Because you have not trusted God for it, and you do not surrender yourself absolutely to God in that trust.

"What is my secret to having fun being saved? My fun being saved used to be an elevator experience: up and down at fast intervals and now I'm learning more of how to die daily in order to have fun being saved daily . . . moment by moment. I believe there are two reasons for this: first, I have been enabled by grace to maintain a good conscience before God day by day: Secondly, I have become a lover of God's Word. A good conscience is unfeigned obedience to God day by day, and fellowship with God every day in His Word, and prayer—that is a life of absolute surrender.

"This is my daily prayer: I give myself absolutely to God, to His Will, to do only what God wants." It is God who will enable me to carry out this surrender. I can't do it alone . . . it is impossible! God is willing to maintain our life. God wants us to be separate from the world; we are called to come out from the world that hates God. Come out for God, and say: "Lord, anything for Thee." If you say that with prayer, and speak that into God's ear, He will accept it and He will teach you what it means.

"You may not have such strong and clear feelings of deliverances as you would desire to have, but if you, like me, have a "want to" in your heart, then humble yourself (my biggest obstacle) in His sight and acknowledge that you have grieved the Holy Spirit by your self-will, self-confidence and self effort. You must deny self once and for all. Denying self must every moment be the power of your life and then Christ will take possession of you. Then the Holy Spirit will bring the whole Christ—Christ crucified and risen and living in glory—into your heart.

Things to Bring About Daily Dying to Self

1. *A Supreme Love For Jesus*
   Self-love is one of the most stubborn hindrances to discipleship. Not until we are willing to lay down our very lives for Him are we in the place where He wants us.
2. *A Denial Of Self*
   "If any man will come after me, let him deny himself. . . ." (Matt. 16:24)
3. *A Deliberate Choosing of the Cross*
   The cross is not some physical infirmity or mental anguish; these things are common to all men. The cross is a pathway that is deliberately chosen.
4. *A Life Spent In Following Christ*
   In order to be His disciples, we must walk as He walked. We must exhibit the fruit of Christ likeness. (John 15:8)
5. *A Fervent Love For All Who Belong to Christ*
   "By this shall all men know that ye are my disciples, if ye have love one to another." (John 13:35)
6. *An Unswerving Continuance In His Word*
   "If ye continue in my word, then are ye my disciples indeed." (John 8:31)
7. *A Forsaking Of All To Follow Him*
   "So likewise, whosoever he be of you that forsaketh not all that he hath, he cannot be my disciple" (Luke 14:33)

REMEMBER: "It is God which worketh in you, both to will and to do". In Romans 7, the regenerate man says: "To will is present with me, but to do—I find I cannot do. I will but I cannot perform." But in Phil. 2, you have a man who has been led on farther, a man who understands that when God has worked the renewed will, God will give the power to accomplish what that will desires."

And so we have the words of a man with a new experience under his belt. He has practiced what he preached. He has taken his own medicine. He has taken his burdens to the Lord. He has given up both himself and his ministry to the Lord.

There really cannot be too many things in life more beautiful, refreshing, or encouraging than to see a big man admit that he has been wrong.

CHAPTER IV

A New Beginning
An Old Conclusion

> 'We are climbing Jacob's Ladder
> We are climbing Jacob's Ladder
> We are climbing Jacob's Ladder
> Soldiers of the Cross
> Every rung goes higher higher
> Every rung goes higher higher
> Every rung goes higher higher
> Soldiers of the Cross'

These words are from a popular religious chorus. Jacob was a servant of God who one night saw a ladder reaching to the sky. The idea behind the song is that a person who serves the Lord just keeps going to higher ground and better things.

Of course, it didn't happen to Jacob that way. In the back of the Thompson Chain Reference Bible there is a chart showing the various experiences that Jacob had as a follower of God. The chart looks more like a rollercoaster than a ladder. For Jacob—who became Israel, the father of the Hebrew nation—had his ups and downs. He was up at Bethel when he made a vow to God. He was down later in his struggle with his father-in-law. Later, he is up again at Peniel when he wrestled with an angel in another memorable spiritual experience. In time, he was down again over trouble with his sons. Then he was back at Bethel, and remembered his earlier experience. But later, more family troubles. And finally, he was close to God and family at his death in Egypt.

I mention this little sermonette because I feel it is true to spiritual development in all persons who seek to do God's will. I mention it because, as you read this chapter in Bob's experience, you are going to think it inconsistent with the previous chapter. In truth, I am convinced this is the way God does things.

One of the first things Bob did upon his return from Washington was to call Ron Sowers, his business manager, Jack Price, his musician, and myself in for a State-of-the-Ministry discussion. It was the first time Bob had been willing to bring me—and the other two for that matter—into a serious decision making conference regarding the future of the ministry.

Jack Price has been with Bob for a little over five years. Jack is a most unusual man. He has the best voice in religious music. In the years to come, he will continue to emerge as one of the top vocalists in America, religious or otherwise. He is also a choir director par excellence. Added to this, he is the kind of great platform man that Bob has to have. Jack's keenest value to Bob is a precise sense of judgment and his total commitment to Bob's ministry.

We took a hard look at the bottom line that day in Bob's office. One of the principal problems was the lack of a reign on expenditures. Expenses could fluctuate as much as ten to twenty thousand dollars in a single month. This could happen because things were often bought or ordered without first finding out the price—or if the price was the best possible. Bob often had a fault of thinking that everyone would naturally look after his own best interests.

By the end of that day, we had not only trimmed some unnecessary costs, but had set up guide-lines whereby no money would be spent beyond what we had budgeted.

The leak had now been stopped in the bottom of the boat. The only question that remained was whether we could ride out the exorbitant costs of television time and production.

February and March sped by. During this time, I was not as close to Bob's picture because I was fighting battles with my own young company. The parent company, Computer Dimensions, of which Church Systems was a subsidiary, was having troubles. I was informed that if my company did not double in size in the next two months, it would be divested. I had made a 700% growth in the company in one year. Now I had to make a 100% improvement over that in 2 months.

In early April, I received a call from Bob. I had never heard him so low. He began by saying, "C. A., I am going to have to get out. I have gone as far as I can go."

I said, "Do you mean you are going to drop your mail?"

"I mean everything," he replied. "TV, mail, *Heartbeat* —everything. I don't have any choice."

"And end up an old man taking up an offering in some local church in Alabama?"

"Maybe you can see a way out, but I cannot. I have borrowed all I can borrow. I am deeper under than ever before."

A chill went through me. "Look, Bob, you have everything on the line; but so do I. I have spent a lot of your money, but I have also put a lot of money into your ministry. If you go down now, so do I. You aren't just making a decision to stop the Bob Harrington Ministry; you are making the decision to shut down my company. You at least owe me the opportunity to take a last look at the alternatives before you put a gun to both our heads."

He told me to meet him the next day in New Orleans. I told him to be ready with a won-loss analysis of the 54 TV stations.

By the time I reached his office, Bob, Jack Price and Ron Sowers had all the numbers ready. We took each station one by one to see what had been spent on that station and what had come in from contributions in each area.

We found that about ten of the stations were paying for themselves or better. We found that 27 of the stations —including the paying 10—were carrying at least 50% of the load and improving.

That left 27 stations that, for 8 months had been bringing in about $100 every time $1,600 was being spent—per station!

The obvious business decision was to cut the 27 poor stations. This idea was repugnant to Bob. It was, for him, like taking 27 books out of the Bible, or, having five children, and putting the two sick ones in an orphan's home.

Cutting the 27 stations would not be enough to offset the acute situation we were in. This would stop an extremely large cash flow, but it would do nothing to make up the lost ground.

We had to get funds from somewhere and the only logical place was a new 40,000 list (not the original one) made up of names of people who had heard Bob in crusades plus ones who had contributed previously through the mail during the past 8 months.

It was also decided that the people had to be told the whole story. I recalled the picture Bob had painted of himself down on his knees begging. I anticipated the difficult time we would have getting him to take this measure, and I was not wrong.

Within an hour, we had sent the letter cutting 27 stations. We spent the rest of the night composing a letter to go to the people. There simply is no more difficult job than this. Such a task is called "burning a list". It is a letter that has to say, "Help me or it's all over."

A dozen times during the night, Bob backed out of the task. In the last analysis, he was won over with a philosophy that I believe with all my heart.

Unfortunately, many men who use the mail resort to cheap gimmicks and huckster-type philosophy. I recently heard a "mail expert" say that three things were essential to an effective mailing: (1.) appeal to selfishness (2.) appeal to emotionalism (3.) Use some gimmick that cannot be refused.

I totally reject these and will get out of the mailing business before I will be a party to them. To the contrary, I offer three alternative aims: (1.) clearly define what you are trying to do for people (needs of society) (2.) state specifically what you need (3.) offer the donor something that will edify your ministry and also edify the donor's spiritual development (donor needs).

In the light of the above three factors, Bob sent the following letter in April:

April 25, 1973

Mr. & Mrs. John Doe
Route 4, P.O. Box 000
Elba, Alabama

Dear Mr. & Mrs. Doe

It breaks my heart to write this letter. To the best of my ability I have run the race and kept the faith. But it now looks as if I may have to take "Chaplain of Bourbon Street" off the television on most if not all stations. This would be like killing a child of my own who was born to do good for Christ. But it appears I have no other choice.

Here are the cold hard facts that I must face. We are on 50 stations. Each month I have been spending $250 per station more than I receive. I am facing a $150,000 deficit. I have held on as long as I can. I simply cannot go any deeper in debt without jeopardizing my entire ministry.

Unless something changes for the better, next month will be the last program in your area. Never have I felt more strongly that something was of God than "Chaplain of Bourbon Street". Never have so many people found courage to try Jesus and face life in my ministry than through "Chaplain of Bourbon Street."

If this program leaves the air I believe the angels will fold their wings and weep and demons will hold a carnival throughout the land. I come to you with this eleventh hour appeal, even for those of you who have stayed with me so faithfully.

For a "Save Chaplain of Bourbon Street" gift of $10 or more, I will send you all of the following: the long playing album, "It's Fun Being Saved", a vest-pocket companion for soulwinning, my own personal testimony, and an 8X10 photograph of the Harrington family. Let me send you this package with my gratitude. Please send at least $10 today. Please hurry!

Gratefully saved

Bob Harrington
saved 4-15-58

P.S. When you write, ask for TV gift number 8.

I have stated previously that a second mailing has to
be planned and sent before the returns from the first come
in. There had been no signs of relief when it was time for
the May letter to go out. The substance of that letter was
as follows:

May 15, 1973

Mr. John Smith
800 Jones St.
Houston, Texas

Dear Mr. Smith

Before you read this letter, read the article in the enclosed *Heartbeat* entitled, "A Heart to Heart Talk
About Television." Then you will understand why my
heart is on fire and my head is spinning with righteous
indignation. Think of it! We had to let go of 27 stations where people were hearing about Jesus! That's
a victory for the devil and I won't stand for it!

Hundreds of you who receive this letter did not see
"Chaplain of Bourbon Street" this month. Thousands
who need Jesus didn't see it. A lost man called me and
asked what happened. What could I tell him? We
Christians have money for everything but souls! I
didn't tell him that. I said, "Just hold on and I'll get that
sermon back in your home."

And I will! When God made me, He made me a
fighter! He made a man who doesn't quit! I don't care
what I have to do, I'm going to find the money to get
Jesus to people like that man who called. I'm preaching now morning, noon and every time the sun goes
down. But if I have to take a part-time job from mid-

night until morning, I'll get the witness for Jesus back on these stations.

Help me! First, by your prayers. Our staff is praying around the clock for this TV burden. Join us in prayer. Second, send a contribution today to help save these 27 stations for Jesus. Please do not wait. Every penny means 2 more people who hear about Jesus. $10 means 2000 souls! Let me hear from you today. And please pray!

If you will help me by sending a "Save Chaplain of Bourbon Street" contribution of $10 or more, I will send you the following: the long playing album, "Old Time Religion", the inspiring booklet, "7 Minutes With God", and a packet of helpful witnessing tracts. Help me beat the devil out of these 27 stations. Please hurry!

Gratefully saved

Bob Harrington
saved 4-15-58

P.S. Write today and ask for TV gift number 7

The above letter referred to an article in the *Heartbeat* which was enclosed with the letter. The *Heartbeat* article said this:

A Straight Talk About T.V.

When you receive this newsletter, many of you will be aware that we are no longer on TV in your area. This past month, we had to drop 27 of our 54 stations. I felt that you needed to know exactly what has been happening and what will be happening in the future.

We began last September with 50 TV stations. I had been saving every extra penny that came to the Bob Harrington Ministry so that I could carry the financial load of the TV stations for six months. I felt this would give time for those of you in the local areas to see the value of the TV witnessing and pick up the burden.

After four months, my savings were gone, but I didn't give up. Joyce and I put up our house and, along with all our ministry assets, borrowed $100,000.

After three more months, that was also gone. But I still wasn't willing to give up. Therefore, this last month, I did not simply keep the stations where the gifts covered expenses. If people in an area were even covering 50% of the costs, I held on for their sake.

If your station went off the air, it was because the station was costing me 3 to 4 times as much as the contributions in the area.

I am sincere when I say that I would keep all the stations even if nothing were coming in if I had the personal resources to do so. But, I now have all my resources invested, and I could not go any deeper in debt and be a good steward of my ministry.

Now, let me share the part that seems strange. We get loads of correspondence from all areas—not just the more solid stations—telling of the miracles God has been performing in lives and homes and businesses. I keep asking myself, "Then why don't more people help?"

Call a group together and join us in prayer for the sake of those who need Christ. Pray for the "Chaplain of Bourbon Street."

Everything was done that could be done. The case now rested with 40,000 human beings who had one thing in common: at some point during the past 8 months, these persons had contributed to Bob's ministry. Whether they would do it again would soon be learned.

During the next two months, my company doubled its revenue. The fact is, that we would have done it even without Bob. He simply made my task easier. Jack Price can make it in any league because he has a great talent. Jack will be the first to admit that Bob has given him a giant head start. But the fact is that Jack is now a highly marketable commodity in the field of religious music. Ron Sowers had already submitted an undated resignation because he is a preacher and wants to preach.

The point is that nobody in that room really had anything to lose but Bob. Had Bob thought only of himself, he could have cut out a satisfactory path for himself easier than anyone in the room.

Bob had more to lose and less to gain than anyone. But he stayed steady in the boat. Why? God only knows why. He wanted to reach his goal of "Every eye and every ear in the Seventies"; he didn't want to fail; he isn't a quitter; he doesn't want to help himself by hurting others; he is a good man and believes in going forward if at all possible. Take your pick. They all lead to the same conclusion:

Where Do We Go From Here?

People have been calling and writing to ask what it would take to get "Chaplain of Bourbon Street" back on the air in their town. Let me answer that question in the following way.

Each station I dropped has been costing about $400 a month more than I was receiving in gifts from each area. Therefore, this is what it would take.

1. Everyone who was giving, continue to give.
2. One person pledge to give $400 per month.
3. Or 40 pledges to give $10 per month.
4. Or 80 pledges to give $5 per month.

So you see, we are not far away from victory on any of the stations.

In the coming weeks, I am—as in the past—going to be dividing all gifts according to the areas from which they were given.

The moment we even begin to get close to a break-even, your station will come back on the air.

If those of you who have been with me will stay with me, we could be only 80 people away from victory—or even only 40—or even one.

I know of one group that is preparing to finance the station in their area.

This is missions if I ever saw it. Do you want the gospel coming to your friends and loved ones as strong as I can give it with God's power?

Then help me. Please examine the enclosed letter carefully. And then ask God to lay on your heart what your part can be.

There was a lot of courage on display on that April day in New Orleans. And it was all coming from the brash, happy-go-lucky offbeat minister from Bourbon Street who was inadvertently carving for himself a place in America's religious history. Someday, people who read these words will marvel that a man so low could reach so high; but that may be the stuff heroes are made of.

Bob at the White House (Phase I).

CHAPTER V

Out of the Frying Pan Into the Fire
WASHINGTON-PHASE I

It was Monday morning, May 14, about 7:00 AM. I was up, but barely, still trying to get in gear for the day and the week—which is the curse of Monday—when my wife called from the den and said Bob wanted me on the phone. My stomach immediately knotted, a habit I had developed ever since the famous "April Phone Booth" call (the "let's call-it-quits" call had been made by Bob from an airport phone booth). And it wasn't that call alone; I had received about 6 phone calls from Bob (although I had called him more often) in the past 6 months and each had been some sort of problem call. Furthermore, the April Phone Booth call had come to my house, as this one now, about 7:00 AM on a Monday morning.

"Hello there," he said in a semi-cheerful voice. This tells you nothing because Bob has a phone pattern that he always follows—at least with me. He leads off with a cheerful salutation, goes into a very serious three or four sentence monologue and then abruptly ends the conversation almost as if someone unexpected entered the room from his end. If perhaps you should speak in response, he hurries you along with some "Uh-huhs."

At any rate, he doesn't waste any of his charm on a phone call. I should complain. Many people tell me I don't say goodby on the phone. I simply hang up. I guess you can see by now I don't get much thrill from talking to Bob on the phone.

"Look, I'm here in Baltimore—Downtown Civic Center —staying at the Holiday Inn across the street. I'm speaking Friday morning to about 1,500 public officials at the Annual Mayor's Prayer Breakfast. I spoke there last year and they liked it—only had 500 last year. Collect your thoughts around that little assignment and come up here about Wednesday. You and I and Jack will talk about the ministry."

"O.K."

"Bye now; everything fine there?"

"Yes."

"By the way, the mail looks good; maybe the best ever —we'll see you, now."

Click.

Click.

What did he mean, "The mail looks good, see you now." How about, "Praise God, thank you, C. A., glory hallelujah!" My Lord in Heaven, what he was saying was that we had been saved! For the first time in eight months we were gaining ground! And he tacks the information on the tail end of a conversation that could have as easily been made at 10 in the morning!

This is not meant as a criticism of Bob, but rather as a clue to understanding this type ministry. A ministry, like a church, is dynamic. It is either growing or dying, but it is never simply holding its own. A ministry must either be in the act of going forward or backward. There is no neutral place where you can do the same thing for the same people with the same people helping you.

This is why many ministers fail. They either think now or yesterday, when they should be thinking tomorrow. A successful man in any field must keep his eyes on the horizon.

Bob has one hand, one eye, one foot, in the future. I do not know if he plays chess but I think he could be good at it.

I learned later that Bob's request on the phone that morning had been far more significant than I realized. He had never before asked someone to think with him about a speech or sermon.

It was almost midnight, Wednesday, May 16. The three of us—Jack Price, Bob and I—had just finished a late dinner. We were in Bob's room. We were talking about Watergate. If you will roll back time and get out old newspapers, you will recall that Watergate, on May 16, 1973, was just catching the public attention in a big way via the Senate Investigating Committee on TV. In fact, it was still early enough in the Watergate episode to be shocking. About all anyone knew, at this time, was that there was something very very rotten in Washington— but they didn't know, as yet, what, and that there were some real real bad guys involved, but they didn't know, as yet, who.

It was a time when a minister could say too much about the political or government dilemma and make a fool of himself. But, if he said nothing, he might as well be in some other business.

This was the subject—or problem—to which we addressed ourselves until 4:00 AM. I began to see, that night in Bob, a sense of history that has increased over the past few months. But it came through to me that night.

Bob would be lying back on the bed, rotating his eyes from Jack to me, then back to Jack. Suddenly, he would jump to his feet and slap his hands together (this scene occurred three times) and say, "God didn't put me right here within 30 miles of the capitol at a time when our government is falling apart for nothing. I've got to say something at this prayer breakfast!"

What he ultimately said at the prayer breakfast you will learn in a few pages, for it was, in substance, what later became his Washington message. For now, let it simply be recorded that Bob Harrington has probably never been more powerful than at that prayer breakfast. He used all the humor and human interest for which he is known. But through it all, he left a chilling impression upon those 1,500.

"Today, everyone of you is enjoying trying to figure out who the real culprits are in Washington. But how many of you have said, 'Oh, God, if this can happen in the highest levels of our government, has it already happened to me? Where have I failed?' "

The effect that Bob had that morning was a little bewildering. He left the people almost stunned. They were not prepared to hear a timely, current message that was both pertinent and genuinely powerful. Bob was not prepared for people to leave in such a silent, serious manner. He had never left people quite this way. And certainly this is understandable. America was just beginning what would prove to be the most unique political upheaval in its history. And Bob Harrington, as though he were a prophet, had been on target all the way.

When I say Bob wasn't prepared for the response, this isn't an understatement. People—men and women—filed past him at the door with tears streaming down their faces. Repeatedly, they said to him, "All America has to hear what you said this morning."

We returned to Bob's room—Jack, Bob and I. We sat

for a time in silence. Occasionally one of us would say, "God, what a meeting that was." Another, "Yea."

Finally, I said, "Bob, our nation needs to hear what you said today."

Jack followed, "If only you could say in Washington what you said here today."

Now, at this point, any other evangelist—I promise you —including Billy Graham—would have said, "Well, let's pray that God will open doors to us in the future to Washington."

Bob got out of his chair and went to the phone.

"Operator, give me the Statler Hilton in Washington, D.C. . . . "Hello, this is Bob Harrington. When is your Grand Ballroom empty for three or four days? . . . "June 26–28? Would you please reserve those three nights for Bob Harrington? Yes, I will send you a check tomorrow. Thank you."

In this way a unique venture was born that would take its place in this strategic moment in America's history. All eyes, at this time, were upon Washington. There was anxiety, if not concern behind most of those eyes. Many of these eyes belonged to ministers. Most of these ministers felt there was a need for God in this hour.

Even Billy Graham would later say, "I would give him (President Nixon) spiritual advice if he asked for it, but he has not asked." Graham had been seeking an invitation from Washington, but had not been able to secure it on his terms. Graham would not settle for anything less than a unified invitation from all religious groups. He could not get it because some of the blacks felt he had been soft regarding racial interests.

Others probably wished they could be in Washington, but did not have the courage or foresight to launch out on their own.

But one man set in motion plans to go to Washington to try to make his voice heard—Bob Harrington. Without budget, or committee, or funds, or any support beyond his own conviction that Washington was where he should be.

For many people—including many of the ministers in Washington—this explanation was not sufficient. What was the *real* reason Bob was going to Washington? Let Bob speak for himself:

Why Am I Going to Washington?

For three nights, June 26-28, I will be preaching the gospel of Jesus Christ in the Grand Ballroom of the Statler Hilton Hotel in Washington, D.C.

This was not on my schedule. I did not plan for it, but God has laid it on my heart to go just as sure as I am alive.

So that you can understand my heart, and pray for Jack Price and myself as we go, let me give a fuller explanation of why I am going and what I hope to accomplish.

   I.   I am going to Washington because I MUST GO.

       1. Only a minister of the gospel can truly understand this fully.

       2. At a certain point in their ministries:

          1.) Jesus said, "I must go to Jerusalem" (though it meant to die)

          2.) Paul said, "I must go to Rome" (though it also meant death)

          3.) Similarly, God has laid on my heart that *now*—at this crucial hour in our nation's destiny—I MUST GO TO WASHINGTON.

  II. I am going to Washington because at this crucial hour God has laid on my heart to make a person to person—face to face—confrontation of the gospel of Christ in our nation's capitol.

1. Our society is daily becoming more impersonal:
   1.) In school—we are a card number.
   2.) On the phone—a circle digit and an area
       code.
   3.) In the mail—a ZIP code
   4.) At work—a social security number
   5.) In sales—a statistic
2. I have a burden to make my personal witness for Christ known face to face in Washington.

III. I am going to Washington because our society
     is on the move and a minister of the gospel must
     stay on the move with the age in which he lives.
     1. Thousands of people migrate and change their
        addresses every day.
     2. More people are born than die every day.
     3. Metropolises are fast becoming megalopolises:
        1.) Over half the nation's population is found
            in 25 population centers.
        2.) Washington is not only one of these 25
            population centers, but is the POWER
            center of our nation's heartbeat.
     4. Therefore, it is natural that a minister who
        is being led both toward where the people
        are and where the action is, will find himself
        gravitating in this hour toward Washington.

IV. I am going to Washington because God—through-
    out history—has moved his ministers toward the
    palace.
    1. Daniel started in a lion's den but ended in the
       King's court.
    2. Joseph started in prison but ended in the
       palace.
    3. Moses started in a basket but ended in the
       King's court.
    4. Nehemiah went into captivity with his people
       —but worked his way to the King's court.

5. Paul used his Roman citizenship plus a death sentence to gain a hearing with the Emperor.
6. Esther used a beauty contest to gain a hearing with the King.
7. All of the prophets of the Old Testament— Ezekiel, Daniel, Jeremiah, Hosea, Jonah—had one thing in common: they were led of God toward the center of national concern in their day.
8. God is leading me at this time—toward the palace.

What Do I Hope to Accomplish?

I. During the past decade, many have said America would go one of three directions:
   1. Toward Chaos—Blow ourselves up.
   2. Toward Communism—Sell ourselves out.
   3. Or Corruption—We would decay from within.
II. We appear—at this hour—to have followed Rome and chosen the third alternative—corruption.
   1. Five reasons were listed for the fall of Rome.
      1.) Immorality
      2.) Drunkenness
      3.) Divorce
      4.) Greed
      5.) DISHONESTY in GOVERNMENT and BUSINESS
   2. You can take those five and write a modern history of America in general and Washington in particular.
III. I propose that God has a fourth alternative— Christian revival—
   1. The other night our President stood with Irving Berlin and sang "God Bless America"
   2. But WHY should God bless America?
      1.) So that she can continue down a toboggan sled of moral and spiritual decay?

       2.) No—God should bless America only if America repents!
   3. "Stand Beside Her and Guide Her."
       1.) But should God stand beside her as she carves out a future designed for destruction?
       2.) No—the future doesn't belong to America —the future belongs to God.
       3.) And God has promised to stand beside those who stand beside him!
IV. Whatever can be accomplished is in God's hands but I must do my part—I MUST TRY.
   1. Recently—regarding Watergate—one person remarked "Why did this happen to us? We didn't do anything."
   2. Maybe that's the trouble—too many of us haven't DONE ANYTHING.
   3. I am going to Washington because I must DO SOMETHING.
       1.) I will preach the righteousness of Jesus Christ without the shackles of partisanship.
       2.) I will uphold the moral standards of God and let the chips fall where they may.
       3.) I will call America to accept two things: Repentance toward God. Faith in the Lord Jesus Christ.
   4. I am not concerned about the results—
       1.) God hasn't called me to get results.
       2.) God has called me to be faithful.
   5. And being faithful for me in this hour includes going to our nation's capitol with the gospel of Christ.

(The above article was published in *Heartbeat* and also released to the press.)

We had five weeks to get ready for Washington and

Bob would be preaching City-Wide Crusades during three of those weeks. We began what became a common occurance during the next few weeks. Bob, Jack and I would get together after a service and talk Washington until almost dawn.

Bob would pace the floor asking the question repeatedly, "What can our going to Washington mean to the cause of Christ?" His answer was finally hammered out, after long discussions, in a second article in *Heartbeat* entitled, "What The Washington Crusade Means to the Cause of Christ."

Penetration

Jesus said go into all the world and preach the gospel. That is our GREAT commission.

Before we can even begin to fulfill it, we must realize that we are surrounded—not by ONE world, but rather a NUMBER OF WORLDS.

Each of these worlds is separate and distinct from the others. Each has its own language, interests and people. There is the world of Business, the world of Athletics, the world of Science, the world of Young People. And there is the World of Government.

Before an outsider can help evangelize one of these worlds for Christ, he must PENETRATE IT! He must get on the inside. And when he finally does penetrate that world, he still can't do it all himself. He must reach people already on the inside for Christ. Then these will witness to their own world for Jesus.

This is why God is leading me to Washington—to penetrate the WORLD OF GOVERNMENT. I know I cannot do it alone for I am not a politician. But I have contacted congressmen, senators, judges, cabinet people who love Christ, and have asked them to join me. And Praise the Lord, many have already said, "Yes, Bob, come and preach the gospel and don't hold any punches!"

I have contacted the ministers of Washington and asked them to join me in this eleventh hour to help penetrate deeper into the suspicion ridden, confused and corrupt world of government.

Many of these preachers have said, "We're with you! Come on."

Establish A Beachhead

You may ask, "Bob, do you think you can win Washington in three days?"

My reply is, "Who knows? God and Jonah did it in Ninevah in ONE DAY!"

But let me make clear that I am not going to try to win all Washington to Christ in three days. I am going to ESTABLISH A BEACHHEAD! I want to get there and run up a flag! Drive down a peg.

If God blesses and honors with His powers and spirit, I will come back to Washington next month— and the next month. Every open time I have for the rest of the year I will RETURN TO WASHINGTON.

Sunday, Ham and Moody used to come to a city and stay weeks, and EVEN MONTHS until the power began to fall and conviction began to come.

If God leads, I am prepared to do just that in Washington. And I know this may not make me popular with the devil—or the National Council of Churches. But GOD IS LEADING ME! I HAVE PRAYED LONG AND HARD ABOUT THIS.

As long as I can keep finding another $500 for another night's rent on the Grand Ballroom, I'll keep going back. I'll rent a room down the street and "Stay til the light breaks through."

Making Myself Available

Pray for me, my dear friend, as I do what I know God wants me to do. He is leading me to make myself available to those in our nation's capitol at this time.

I confess to you I do not know at this time how I

will finance this endeavor, but God will provide, because it is right and good. I believe you will help me as you have in the past. Send a gift today, if you can, and by all means pray.

Here is my prayer for Washington:

"Lord, set me on fire—and then call our government leaders out to WATCH ME BURN!"

Bob sent the ministers of Washington D.C. area both of these articles ("Why I AM Going" and "What It Can Mean") along with this cover letter!

Dear Reverend Arnold

God has laid it on my heart to come to Washington and preach at this time. I am enclosing a fuller explanation of my feelings which have prompted this action.

I have scheduled the Grand Ballroom of the Statler Hilton Hotel for the nights of June 26-28. I need your help and am earnestly requesting your support in the effort to make a witness for Jesus Christ.

Let me quickly say that I am not trying to undermine, but rather to complement the good job you men are doing.

And you are doing a good job! It takes guts to be a minister in the nation's capitol. You are the men who carry the ball in Washington. You're the men who stay up all night at the hospital and return to your office to battle through the next day.

Now I know I talk fast, and your people probably wouldn't have me as their pastor. But I do have a different voice, and maybe it could help a little at this time.

We are asking senators, congressmen and national figures who love the Lord to join us. Walter Brennan will be with us on Tuesday night.

I need the support of you and your people. Will you let me help? Will you help me? I am enclosing a card. I would greatly appreciate your response. And when you come, please let me know you are there. I want the ministers with me at the front and on the platform.

Thank you for your consideration of this matter.

Gratefully saved

Bob Harrington

Along with the letter and articles, Bob sent this card.

God Bless America Rally
June 26-28
Washington, D.C.

Bob:

☐ I will announce this to my people and urge their attendance
☐ I will attend Tuesday night
☐ I will attend Wednesday night
☐ I will attend Thursday night
☐ I will try to come all nights

signed _____

You should contact: Name _____

Address _____

Telephone _____

Two ministers bothered to return the card. A few others finally supported the crusade. But the overriding attitude of 9 out of 10 ministers in the area was, "Who does he think he is coming up here into our territory." Oh hum.

A rush was placed on the July mailing so that the following letter could be received by all on Bob's mailing list prior to June 26.

June 15, 1973

Dear Joann

Please read the enclosed *Heartbeat* from cover to cover. It describes the greatest challenge God has ever laid on my heart. I am going to Washington, D.C. to preach the gospel. No one has invited me but the Lord. But our nation needs a revival now as never before and it must begin in Washington.

I have not had time to make plans or raise a budget, but I must go. Jesus said He had to go to Jerusalem. Paul said he had to go to Rome. And I must go to Washington to preach the righteousness of Jesus Christ.

I tried to pick out the closest spot I could find to the capitol, and it turned out to be the Grand Ballroom of

the Statler Hilton Hotel. The only available nights
were June 26-28, and I took them. Will you help me
reach our nation's capitol for Christ? I am going to ask
you to send an offering to help with the expenses. The
Ballroom alone costs $500 per night. Maybe God will
lead you to provide one night's rent.

Some have told me I should wait until I get the full
support of the churches, or until I could raise the funds
to cover the costs. I can't wait. The devil isn't waiting
to bring our nation into moral chaos. And I must go to
Washington now to preach the righteousness of Christ.
Please help me.

If you will send a gift of $10 or more for the God
Bless America Crusade, June 26-28, I am going to send
the following: (1) A long-playing album of our first
TV show, including both music and sermon (2) A
handbook helpful to you as a soul winner (3) One
dozen "It's Fun Being Saved" stickers. Please help me.
All gifts this time will be used for the God Bless
America Washington Crusade. Please hurry, and Pray.

Gratefully saved

Bob Harrington

P. S. When you write, ask for TV offer #2

Anyone can go to Washington for the price of an air
ticket. The trick is to make a splash. Washington is like
no other city in the United States, beginning with the fact
that it isn't a city, but a district—with Virginia and Maryland confusing the picture from two directions.

Washington has absolutely no unifying force. Top levels of government exist away from the public eye as

though from another planet. Various levels of bureaucracy plod along unmindful of each other. It is a city without a heart; a city of crime and violence; a city where it is impossible for a person to gain a sense of belonging for the city has no center. Mythological giants float in and out of the building called the Capitol; blacks fill the streets, slums and jails; the rich fill the mansions on the Virginia hillsides. Tens of thousands of clerical people daily go their lonely ways to their lonely jobs.

There is literally no cohesiveness to the place; a wasteland for a Chamber of Commerce or a Community Center. It is a good place to go to run for President, run from the police, or commit suicide.

There is no such thing as rallying the forces in Washington, for there is no common tongue, goal, ideology, plight, or interest. It is a city that crushes hope; truly the most exciting city in all the world in which to spend one day.

Bob's plans were to spend three. Oh, when visions of sugar plums danced in his head, he could dream of seeing congressmen and senators flooding into the Statler's Grand Ballroom; and the President calling for a private counsel. In the light of day, he knew he was more likely biting off a lonely, possibly even isolated three days for himself.

We began shopping for all the help we could get. Larry Coyle, of Coyle Advertising in Los Angeles, helped secure Walter Brennan for the first night. Larry is a truly great person, a dear friend and also a business partner of mine. He also happens to be one of Walter Brennan's closest friends.

Walter's normal fee for a personal appearance is $10, 000. He happens to be a man with a deep religious commitment and an even deeper sense of patriotism. What Bob was attempting appealed to him and he consented to come across America to participate in the God Bless America Crusade free.

The first night, June 26, the Ballroom was filled to its 1,000 seat capacity. Walter all but stole the show. He proved the trooper he really is. He has emphysema so badly that he has to fight for every breath of air. We had to put him in a wheel chair to get him from place to place in the big hotel without completely losing his breath.

However, the moment Bob called him to the platform, Walter became the performer, the star. He began pumping his arms like he was doing the Funky Chicken as he broke into his famous prance toward the stage. Seventy-nine years old!

After he finished bringing a word of testimony and greeting, Walter returned to sit beside me down front. He had never heard Bob speak. He was not prepared for what he heard. After Bob had been going about 15 minutes, Walter turned to me and said, "He's dynamite! This man could have made it to the top in Hollywood, and still could. He has a sense of humor and a sense of timing. He's dynamite!"

After the service, Walter was as moved as he was impressed. At Bob's request, he returned to the platform where he stood beside Bob and prayed along with those who had accepted Christ. Walter's Catholic background had not conditioned him for such public display of personal faith in Christ. He decided, that night, that It Was Fun Being Saved.

What some people think Bob resorts to out of laziness, he actually does by design. He repeats himself. Instead of trying to say something completely new each time he speaks, Bob often takes a theme and drives it home again and again. The following material was the basic content from which he spun his several Washington messages:

HERE IS BOB HARRINGTON'S
WASHINGTON MESSAGE
PRAY FOR BOB JUNE 26-28

Three Alternatives

A decade ago, it was being said that America would soon meet destruction in one of three ways:

CHAOS: Some thought there would be a Nuclear War and we would blow ourselves up. And many of us can recall the night the Russian ships were headed for Cuba and President Kennedy had drawn the line. We came within a prayer and a nuclear hair of chaos.

COMMUNISM: In the early sixties, the Communists had announced their plan for world domination. Their target date for taking over the United States was 1973!

CORRUPTION: There were others who were saying, like Spengler, that America would decay morally from within.

Here we are in 1973. We have not blown ourselves up. We have not sold out to Communism. But we are experiencing the climax of the greatest moral crisis in our nation's history.

We were indifferent to crime in the streets. We were embarrassed but not really shocked by the dope and sex trips of young people.

But when corruption finally broke into the open in the top levels of our government, we were appalled. Where do we go from here?

Split Level Society

Years ago in America, there was a two story attitude toward right and wrong. We knew right from wrong.

Today, we have brought right so far down, and wrong so far up, that we don't know which is which!

And it isn't just in government. This split level attitude toward right and wrong is in all parts of our society.

IN TELEVISION—it took the form of payola on quiz programs. The strange thing about this was that America was divided on whether this was right or wrong.

IN SPORTS—it became point shaving. Athletes were told to win, but not by very much!

IN INDUSTRY—major company representatives began meeting in hotels to decide who would get the next bid on a big job. The result was that leading citizens spent a year in jail.

IN GOVERNMENT—we have now seen take place what has been called A Twilight of Honor. This refers to a book several years ago where an older lawyer was telling a younger lawyer how to succeed in government. He said, "Son, you have to have two souls. One must be filled with idealism and a sense of right. Use this one in the public places. But out there in the world of ambition, self interest and survival, you must have a SECOND SOUL THAT CAN BE SOLD!

What Have We Lost in America?

1. WE HAVE LOST OUR SENSE OF DIRECTION —The prophet Jeremiah said that the people of his day came under the judgment of God because they went backward and not forward.

   Recently in Miami, a young man was trying to set a new record for depth diving. The charts showed that he did it. But he never came up. Later his body was found in another part of the ocean.

   The boy had fallen victim to the CALL OF THE DEEP. He got down where everything looked the same. And when he started to surface, he thought DOWN was UP and went down to his death.

   This is what the prophet Jeremiah would say to America today. We have kept shaving away at right until we today are calling wrong right—and backward forward—and down up—and false true —We have lost our sense of direction.

2. WE HAVE LOST OUR SENSITIVITY—We are blind to our own sins. What do you hear people say about Watergate? Something like, "Why did they do that; or, it serves them right; or, I thought those people were like that."

   But how many of us have stopped and asked, "Oh, God, what is there in my own life that is wrong and needs to be made right?"

3. WE HAVE LOST OUR FEAR OF GOD—The Bible says, "The wages of sin is death." BUT THAT DOESN'T WORRY AMERICA.

   The Bible says, "Broad is the road that leads to destruction, but narrow is the road that leads to life." BUT THAT DOESN'T WORRY AMERICA.

   But, my friend, we better START BELIEVING IT. Because God has never let another nation off the immoral, sinful hook, and He won't let us either. And on every page of the Bible, God has said He will not let a nation, or a community or an individual TAKE A WRONG ROAD AND REACH A RIGHT DESTINATION!

Is There Hope?

America has only one ray of hope—to REPENT. And that means to return to the RIGHTEOUSNESS of Jesus Christ.

We have called ourselves a Christian nation, yet we have not acted like it. We would not try to take the sun without its brightness, but we have tried to have CHRIST WITHOUT HIS RIGHTEOUSNESS.

Is it too late for America? I do not know. We may, as a nation, have gone too far or waited too long so that we have become numb to the call of God.

But I know this. WE BETTER TRY.

Bob and Walter discussing the Bible in Washington (Phase I).

Bob pauses to pray for the nation's capitol (Phase I).

Bob and Jack prayerfully express concern for the man who lives in this house.

Walter Brennan giving his testimony in Washington (Phase I).

Walter Brennan, Bob, and Senator Strom Thurmond at Statler
Hotel, Washington (Phase I).

Bob preaching to capacity crowd on his first trip to Washington.

Walter Brennan, Bob, and Senator Thurmond at a service in the Statler Ballroom, Washington. Those in front are responding to the invitation.

One other fact should be noted before we look at the highlights of the first Washington trip, such as they were. When the idea of going to Washington first came up, Bob said this:

"I am not interested in a quickie trip to Washington. We cannot whip the world in one day. If we go at all, we are going to make plans to go several times and try to build momentum. Therefore, before Bob made trip one to Washington, he had made reservations for trips two and three.

The following report, which appeared in the August *Heartbeat*, summarizes the key events of Washington Phase I:

BEACHHEAD ESTABLISHED IN WASHINGTON, RETURNING SEPTEMBER 25-27

Special Report, Washington—Phase I

We went to Washington June 26-28 with your prayers, financial support and personal participation in order to establish a beachhead; in order to begin a work for God that would grow and grow until it reached the heights and depths and length and breadth of this most strategic nerve center of our entire nation.

My report to you is that your *prayers paid off!* Your investment was the greatest you have ever made for God and Country.

My *plea* to you is to stay with me for *we have just begun.* Because space is brief and I have so much to share with you, let me simply highlight the events of the three days.

  I. *TUESDAY—JUNE 26*

    1. *NOON*—I preached to the World Prayer Fellowship.

      1.) This group is headed by Mr. Doug Coe and is responsible for planning the President's Prayer Breakfast each year.

      2.) This group pledged total support in all our future endeavors.

      3.) The Korean was present who set up Billy Graham's Korea Crusade. He said he could do the same for me.

      4.) A Three Star General was present at noon and made a public decision for Christ Tuesday night!

    2. *Night*—Hundreds filled the Statler Ballroom.

      1.) Buses came from Baltimore.

      2.) Others drove hundreds of miles to be present.

      3.) Walter Brennan flew across the country to

speak a word for God and Country.

    4.) Senator Strom Thurmond came to the platform to bear witness to his faith in Christ and his support of our efforts.

  3. Standing Tuesday night before congressmen, military leaders, and with Walter Brennan at my side weeping tears of joy, I knew we had landed and the beachhead was on its way!

II. *WEDNESDAY—JUNE 27*

  1. *8:00* AM—I spoke at the Congressional Prayer Breakfast inside the House of Representatives.

    1.) Among those present was Fishbait Miller, the Doorkeeper of the House. He said to the press, "Bob Harrington always draws the biggest crowds to any House Event . . . they respect his power with God."

    2.) We received an invitation to speak for the main Congressional Prayer Breakfast in January.

  2. *10:00* AM—We were guests for an hour in the White House.

    1.) We watched the historic hearings of John Dean with the head of the White House F.B.I.

    2.) While John Dean pointed to corruption in high places, we stood at the open door to the Oval Office and prayed that God would lead us to keep pointing to His righteousness in higher places.

    3.) The President was in San Clemente. He will be back, and so will we. The day will come, you mark it down, when I will kneel with our President by that Oval Office sofa. Other's have his ear; I want his heart.

  3. *12:00* NOON—I was a guest on *Panorama,* the most influential talk show in Washington.

      4. *Night*—Another 100 found Christ in the Ball-
room.
III. *THURSDAY—JUNE 28*
    1. *Noon*—I spoke to a large group in the prayer
chapel at the Pentagon.
      1.) This chapel was opened by Melvin Laird.
      2.) Mr. Laird has pledged his support to our
future efforts.
    2. *Night*—A climactic service at the Statler Ball-
room.
      1.) We announced our return for Washing-
ton—Phase II, September 25-27 at Constitution Hall, a 3,800 seat complex just
blocks from the Capitol.
      2.) Congressman Vinegar Bend Mizell gave
his testimony for Christ.
    3. The Beachhead was established. With your
prayers and continued support, we have just
begun.
      1.) To make Phase II a success, we must now
pray as though it all depends on God and
work as though it all depends on you and
me.
      2.) We could not have paid for Phase I with-
out your generous gifts through the mail.
      3.) Our plans for Phase II are twice as large
as Phase I. Please let me hear from you
soon. Be generous, and pray! We are on
our way!

Everything in the above article is more or less true. It
would be ridiculous for me to infer that it is untruthful
since I helped write it. However, I think there should be
further explanation made at this point in order to under-
score two facts: 1.) The tremendous difficulty in attempt-
ing this type venture. 2.) The progress that will become
evident in the second trip to Washington.

Bob did visit the White House, but as the guest, not of the President, but the White House Barber, Jack Allen. He did speak at a Congressional Prayer Breakfast inside the Capitol. However, it must be said in all candor that the breakfast was not packed with senators and congressmen. He did speak to a noon prayer group inside the Pentagon. However, the chapel was located in an almost remote area and was not as large as could have been hoped. And, let's face it; 1,000 people gathered in a hotel Ballroom is not to be considered an overpowering gathering quantitatively speaking.

Even these details, however, must be seen from another perspective. One thousand people coming out at night to downtown Washington is a considerable feat according to Washington standards. Downtown Washington is a dangerous place after dark, especially for unescorted women. An automobile is an open target at night in this urban area.

And as far as the White House, the Capitol and the Pentagon are concerned, the point is that Bob was there trying. He repeatedly stated that he came for a witness; to get his foot in the door; to show his concern; and to say something that the nation needed to hear—and that would be repeated often—that gained significance because of where Bob was when he was making his statement—at the mouth of the gun—at the center of national concern.

I suspect Paul drew relatively little public attention when he went to Rome. Even his execution was an appallingly private affair when viewed in retrospect.

A man qualifies for the role of prophet to the extent that he is willing to take the burden of his nation's religious welfare and bear it with concern, dedication and disregard for personal gain.

Washington, Phase I was a financial drain for Bob. He knew this would probably be the case, and he was not disappointed. An evangelist cannot stay in business if he makes a practice of spending money he knows he cannot recover. Conversely, his ministry will become bland and toothless if an evangelist allows risk—or the lack of it— to dictate his movements.

Herein is the difference that makes Bob an unusual and effective evangelist. By all human standards, this Washington trip was a bad deal from the start. It was destined to draw criticism from local ministers and religious groups, cost a lot of money and achieve relatively small results.

But keep in mind that more attention—serious, almost frantic attention—was being drawn to our nation's capitol at this time than possibly at any other time in our history. The Republic was apparently coming apart at the seams.

This being the case, it should not be considered strange or suspicious that a minister chose to go to Washington and "do his part." It is more strange that every church in America did not enter into a time of special prayer. It would have seemed far more reasonable that ministers by the thousands would storm the capitol for a testimony. The blacks did it in behalf of prejudice; young people did it in behalf of peace; why not ministers in behalf of the Prince of Peace?

This was no mere political quagmire in which our nation was wallowing. This was a dilemma, the greatest ever for our nation, that was inherently and essentially moral at its core.

There are those few incidents in the passing of time that are so unforgettable that one tends to recall where he was when the event took place. Where were you when you received word that President Kennedy had been shot? Your money will be refunded on this book (by the publisher, I hope) if you cannot remember.

I am quite sure that many of us will ask ourselves in the coming years, "Where was I when a man named John Dean accused the President of the United States of criminal activity on national television?"

Bob was in Washington.

CHAPTER VI

A Serious Thing Happened In Fun City LAS VEGAS

To say the first trip to Washington was a drain on Bob would grossly understate the case. He was totally and completely exhausted. But more than the physical, he was emotionally washed out; a frustration borne of giving so much of himself for so apparently little. He put it this way on the way to the plane:

"I don't want to compare myself to Jesus, but I think I understand what He meant when He said, 'Oh, Jerusalem, Jerusalem, how often would I have gathered you to me and you would not come!'

"I have been here three days and didn't really lay a glove on this place. Most of those big men in big places, and those little people in little places, didn't even know we were here trying—or at least didn't care."

I fully expected him to add that Washington could slide into the Potomac for all he cared. When we reached the airport, he phoned Constitution Hall to make sure the dates of September 25–27 were confirmed for his return to Washington.

This is strange. It represents something in Bob's nature that I do not fully understand. There is a twilight zone

that occasionally surfaces in his personality that lies somewhere between being a fighter and using poor judgment.
Let's face it; he did not fill the Statler Ballroom. Oh, they
told us it would hold a thousand, and I did count one
thousand on two different nights.

But there were empty seats in the rear; not many—
maybe 50—but they were there.

And what does he do as he leaves? Schedules a gor-
geous, austere, historical barn downtown that seats 3,800
—four times as many as the Ballroom he just left.

I have alluded to Bob's crowd pulling ability. It is a
strength of his that he can get people to come and keep
coming back—with their friends—just because they enjoy
Bob. Often, however, a person's strength is also his weak-
ness—or can become such. It had become a fetish for Bob
to rent the biggest place in any city and then kill himself
trying to fill it single-handedly.

Bob was on his way to Las Vegas where he was scheduled to speak for eight nights in the large Las Vegas Convention Center right in the heart of "The Strip."

How would you guess that this engagement became a
reality? You might imagine that the ministerial association invited him, or a group of local churches, or even one
church.

You would be wrong. He invited himself. He rented
the Convention Center himself. Then, he called Ted Kerber, Head of the Las Vegas Rescue Mission and asked him
to be chairman of the crusade.

Don't misunderstand. I am not suggesting there were
no ministers at all who were willing to cooperate. A few
did from the start and many more before the week was
over. But there simply is no way for two or three preachers in Las Vegas to bring themselves to rent the Convention Center in the middle of that smallest piece of real

estate in America where the most people have come for one thing: fun.

In the first place, there aren't that many churches in Las Vegas. The city directory lists about 40 and half of those are little, all night chapels where couples come for a quickie wedding. In the second place, the few legitimate churches that exist in Las Vegas are not large.

Let's face it. The tremendous growth in Las Vegas over the past two decades did not happen as the result of a spiritual awakening. The temples of God in this city have no way to compare themselves to the neon-lined temples of greed that literally light the desert for their prey.

I know preachers. I've been one. I've been President of a group of 35,000 of them. And I promise you there is not another minister in America who: 1.) Without any guarantee of financial support 2.) without any guarantee of local church support—would take the risk of renting the huge Las Vegas Convention Center and come in for eight nights. This would be 10% humiliation and 90% financial suicide.

Bob did it. And, at this point, I am not offering this as praise for Bob. This kind of thing was killing his health. He felt somehow he had to do it, but he didn't and later recognized a better way.

But he did it in Las Vegas, and came up smelling like a rose.

Why did he do it? Let him speak for himself. The following statement comes from Bob's August *Heartbeat:*

How far is it from Washington to Las Vegas? About 3,000 miles as the plane flies. But the distance is greater than that for they are worlds apart.

1. One is dedicated to the world of government and the other to the world of fun.
2. The problem is that government isn't much fun these days in Washington and fun isn't much fun in Las Vegas.
3. Some think they could have more fun in Washington if they had more power, and those in Las Vegas think they could have more fun if they had more money.
4. Both are wrong. It's my task to penetrate both these worlds with the message that IT'S FUN BEING SAVED!

We cannot waste time. We have been concentrating recently on Washington, but we are seeking to Wake Up America for Christ!

We are, therefore, going to Las Vegas for these reasons:

1. To burden the hearts of talented people to use their talents for Christ to help Wake Up America.
2. Because this capitol of the world of fun isn't what it is cracked up to be. We are going to Las Vegas to show where the fun really is.
    1.) I know what I'm talking about because I serve on Bourbon Street.
    2.) You may read about the glitter and thrills of sin—Las Vegas style—but that's not the real picture.
    3.) Just as it is on Bourbon Street, I have seen the moral bankruptcy of Las Vegas. It is a city filled with loneliness, heartbreak and despair.
    4.) No city in America points more clearly to the wages of sin than Las Vegas.
    5.) We are not going there to condemn but to spend eight nights in Convention Center preaching the positive, hope-filled message that IT'S FUN BEING SAVED.

Bob arrived for the first service and found two things: about one thousand people waiting to hear him and a deficit of almost $10,000.

Bob has been criticized for being an X-rated preacher. The reason is that he talks like an X-rated preacher; walks like an X-rated preacher; goes to X-rated places; mixes with X-rated people and sometimes even laughs at X-rated fun. I don't know if all this is because he is not enough preacher or too much man, but it does explain why he is criticized for being X-rated in his approach.

You may as well take the voice from a singer, or the toe from a dancer, or the arm from a pitcher, as to try to rob a man of the style that makes him what he is.

Bob Harrington will never be enough preacher for most other preachers. He lives one step from hell because, he thinks, that's where the most sinners are. His words, actions and morals will always be open to ridicule, suspicion and criticism from the more righteous.

But it was his style—not his robe, or short hair, or correct grammar, or his out-of-touch-with-the-worldliness—it was his style that shook the neon bushes of Las Vegas.

That first night, after the service, he called the newspaper, the television stations, the radio stations, and said: "I'm going to go check out a few clubs. Why don't you join me?"

Then he called a nightclub owner and said, "I'm going to drop by and say hello. I'm the Chaplain of Bourbon Street. I won't come to condemn, just bring a few minutes of good clean fun."

The club owner replied, "I don't want any preacher messing up my act. Don't bother to come because I won't let you in."

To which Bob responded, "That's certainly your right, sir, but would you mind stepping outside at 11:00 o'clock

Bob in meditation by day, preparing for the Las Vegas Crusade by night.

Bob on the strip during the Las Vegas Crusade.

Bob in Las Vegas with the Word of God.

and explaining to the radio and television people why you
aren't going to let me in?"

After a long pause, the owner said, "Come on in. I
don't want those people on my back."

Bob went to two clubs in one night. And he did bring
good clean fun. But don't get the idea he was having fun.
We were driving around waiting for 11:00 o'clock. We
passed the club. The TV men were there with camera and
lights.

As we passed, Bob said, "This is the hardest thing I
do in my entire ministry. This takes more out of me than
fifty sermons."

Later, I saw what he meant. I saw him mount a stage
just as a topless-bottomless girl walked off. All lights,
including the new ones of the TV men, were on him. The
place was packed with people into their fourth or fifth
drink, and the air filled with smoke.

As he spoke, one man stood at Bob's feet and shouted
a popular obscenity then turned and walked away.

As we left, several drunks accosted him on the sidewalk,
hurling blasphemies at him. I actually feared for his life.
We formed a circle around him. I wanted him out of
there—fast!

Bob vetoed me. He said, "Let them have their say; I
had mine. Let me try to answer their questions as best I
can."

Whatever "cool" is, I saw it in action on that sidewalk.
Whatever "Christian grace and compassion" are, they had
to be on display in the Chaplain.

One man said, "Tell me, Reverend, aren't you here
just to promote your meeting and make a buck?"

Bob softly, very softly replied, "How do you want me
to answer that, Sir?"

The man stammered, and said, "Well, just tell the truth."

Bob said, "Well, the truth is that I do hope you will come to my crusade; and I do hope we can pay our bills. But I'm here mainly because I was afraid you wouldn't come, and because you think you're having fun doing what you're doing and I wanted you to know I'm having fun knowing Jesus."

The man rocked on his heels, looked long at Bob and put out his hand saying, "Well, if that's how you feel, I'm glad you came. And I just may surprise you and come hear you."

We returned to the hotel where we were supposed to have dinner. Instead, Bob went straight to his room, threw up, and fell into bed.

I heard a sermon one time entitled, "I Sat Where He Sat." The point was, don't ever criticize another person until you have been in his shoes. Some people—mainly fellow ministers—would do well to withhold their judgment, on the brash, X-rated, shallow Chaplain of Bourbon Street until they have stood where he stands.

The next day the various news media—including radio and TV—carried reports of Bob's night. Then the media began calling Bob for interviews. Without giving details, let me simply report that Bob was on both radio and TV in some instances twice every day for the rest of the week. I added it up and determined that Bob got about $100,000 worth of radio and TV advertisement during the eight days—FREE! To him, that made the pain and humiliation of a "night out on the town" worth it.

Beginning Monday night, something truly beautiful began to happen that mere numbers don't adequately convey. It was the quality of the crowd.

First, the numbers: Sunday night, 1,000; Monday night, 2,000; Tuesday through Saturday, 3,000 nightly; Sunday night, 5,000.

Bob and Jack in Las Vegas going to the mission field of new converts.

Bob in front of the Las Vegas Convention Center.

Bob turns the Convention Center into the Tabernacle at Las Vegas.

Now the beauty. First, there was the recognition that there were thousands of people in Las Vegas who were interested in the things of God. Part of the thrill was observing their recognition of each other. I'm sure many of these people had convinced themselves that not a handful in Fun City cared about living for Jesus Christ.

The beauty went even deeper. One had to ask "Who were these people?" Theye were plain ordinary people, just like anywhere else—that's the beauty! Oh, many of them happened to work in bars and clubs. Some were clerks, secretaries and bellmen. Others were dealers, pit bosses, waitresses and bartenders. But they were also husbands and wives, mothers and fathers. They mowed lawns and watched football on TV.

Many were victims of bad luck. Many had come to Fun City to find a castle and had been forced, by circumstances, to settle for a toolshed. In the land of make-believe, they had found fool's gold at the end of their rainbow.

Bob told them it was fun being saved. And then he did a strange thing. He didn't tell them to leave their jobs in their "dens of iniquity." He told them to go back to their bars and casinos, and turn them into mission fields.

Daily, Bob and Jack visited their "friends in Christ" in their mission fields. There was laughter, and real Christian fellowship going on from the Stardust out to the Tropicana; from the Dunes to the Golden Horseshoe. It really did seem like it was fun being saved.

There were over one thousand decisions for Christ during the week. In the closing service, the Christians of Las Vegas contributed a considerable love offering for Bob's second trip to Washington. Let Bob sum it up.

If ever praise was in order, it is with regard to Las Vegas. From start to finish, what happened in Las

Vegas was a clear cut demonstration of the power of the Spirit of God. There simply is no other explanation.

To help you grasp what God did, let me explain certain factors.

1. Millions of dollars each year are spent in this city to buy the time and presence of people.
    1.) A hotel will easily spend $50,000 for an entertainer for one week.
    2.) That hotel will be more than pleased if, during that week, 10,000 people come to the hotel to hear the entertainer.
    3.) Obviously, the goal of the hotel is to get people to spend money gambling.
2. We averaged over 3,000 in attendance every night at the Las Vegas Convention Center (right in the heart of the Strip and next door to the Hilton Hotel where Elvis does his thing.)
    1.) Think of it—over 25,000 (5,000 the last night) in one week in the Sin Capitol of America!
    2.) On purely human terms, what was happening in the name of Jesus at Convention Center was, by far, *the biggest attraction in town.*

But the real story of July 22-29—Las Vegas—was not human but *Divine!* The key to the week was not *People,* but *Power!*

God's Spirit fell every night!

Every night hundreds of persons poured down the aisles to find Christ. The Christians of this city were admittedly bewildered for like the Church of Corinth, they are overwhelmed by the gigantic temples of sin that surround them.

It was not surprising to me for several reasons:

1. I come from Bourbon Street and know the despair and emptiness that lurks at the bottom of Sin—Las Vegas Style.
2. And through Bourbon Street, I have come to

Bob at work.

Hundreds come forward in response to the invitation at Las Vegas.

Praise the Lord for Las Vegas. God's people are the biggest attraction in town.

understand the scripture, "where sin does
abound, grace does *much more abound.*"
3. Most of all, I knew there were thousands of
people all over America—people who write me
regularly and contribute concretely—who were
praying; praying for a *demonstration*—not of the
talent of Bob Harrington—but of the *Power* of
the *Holy Spirit!*

Beachhead Established

For the benefit of those of you who are praying and
pulling and paying with us in our WAKE UP AMER-
ICA Crusade, let me summarize Las Vegas. We didn't
go merely to spend one week, but to establish a Beachhead for the future.
1. Our first victory was to trust God enough to go
in the first place.
1.) We had no invitation to go to Las Vegas
from anyone but God—which was sufficient.
2.) In fact, we were told by dozens we were crazy
to go, and given a dozen reasons why.
3.) Our "committee" was made up of four persons:
Ted Kerber, Head of the Las Vegas Rescue
Mission, and the Father, the Son, and the Holy
Spirit! Praise the Lord!
2. Our second victory was the one thousand new
Christians left behind.
1.) These are continuing the process of *penetra-
tion.*
2.) They have gone back to their casinos, hotels
and bars to witness to their world about Jesus.
3. Our third victory was the way God opened the
media to us.
1.) Every day we were invited to appear on
radio and television.
2.) By the end of the week, arrangements had
been finalized for "Chaplain of Bourbon

Street" to appear on Las Vegas Channel 13 at 8:30 AM *every Sunday morning* from now on!

4. The fourth victory was that Las Vegas Convention Center released to us the date of August 18-25, 1974! We are going back!

5. The fifth victory was that, by the last night, our platform was filled with ministers lending their support.

Reverend Daryl Evenson, Pastor of the First Southern Baptist Church (who was with us all week) said it this way, "The ice has been broken. We will begin praying now for next year. By next August, we will have 10,000 each night to hear Bob."

That's what we are asking of God for America today. Everywhere I go I say three things:

1. Jesus sent me to you.
2. It's Fun Being Saved.
3. I'll Be Back!

"Praise the Lord for Las Vegas, Phase I." (Reprinted from *Heartbeat*—Sept. 1973).

And so you have the refreshing story of Las Vegas, a pleasant episode in Bob's hills and valley year of 1973. Bob accomplished what, I am convinced, no other minister could have accomplished in this city at this time.

I am certainly not contending that all ministers should be like Bob Harrington. Neither am I saying that other ministers should try to make Bob Harrington conform to their image. I am saying there is plenty of room for everyone. And God knows there is no abundance of men trying to do God's work.

If Thoreau will forgive me I will summarize something he said. If a man does not walk in step with others, it is because he hears the beat of another drummer. Let each man walk to the beat he hears, however measured, or far away.

Las Vegas was different. Bob Harrington is different. *Viva la difference!*

CHAPTER VII

Crusades and Television
A Marriage Made
IN SAN DIEGO

Most high school annuals contain, usually full page near the center, a set of "Best" pictures: best looking; best personality; best student; and, finally, best all-around, whatever that means.

San Diego was Bob's Best-All-Around Crusade of 1973. One hundred thousand attended during the eight nights. There were two thousand decisions. There were thirteen thousand people present on the opening night, and Bob has the capacity and ability to sustain the kind of attendance he starts with throughout a week.

In San Diego, Bob didn't have to rely solely on his own resources. He had the rare assistance of over 80 churches actively supporting the crusade. Ivan Sisk, Director of the San Diego County Association of Evangelical Churches, was the crusade Chairman, and did a superb job.

The most significant factor about the San Diego crusade was that it represented Bob's maiden voyage in taking his television remote, and filming the actual crusade services. This single step will, I am convinced, prove to be the most fruitful decision in Bob's ministry to this

129

point, although it has presented more difficulties than can
be described.

During the month preceding San Diego, I met with
Bob in New Orleans to discuss the progress of his television program, "Chaplain of Bourbon Street." Each week
Bob gets a computer print-out which shows the mail response by television stations. After one year, it was evident
that interest in the nightclub format had reached a peak
and was declining.

In the outset, the idea of Bob preaching in a simulated
bar with a mock audience was fresh and different. It high-
lighted the uniqueness of the man who was actually the
Chaplain of Bourbon Street.

Over a period of time, however, a sameness had crept
into the programs. You had the feeling that if you had
seen one, you had seen them all. Furthermore, there was
a sterility in Bob's delivery which was understandable. He
would spend weeks out preaching to real live people and
then return to New Orleans for a marathon taping session
in the studio. The audience was always staff members,
family and close friends of the ministry. The format was
always well orchestrated; the time kept by the second;
the make-up in place.

There was nothing inherently wrong with this approach
for awhile. Other men had used it quite effectively, as did
Bob. Bob would work hard at gearing himself for the people who would ultimately see the program across the
nation.

But a couple of things were wrong with it for Bob.
First, the tapings always caught him when he was tired
and when he should have been getting a bit of rest. Second, the poised precise Bob, with make-up in place was
not Bob. Bob is Bob when his tie is loose, sweat streaming
down his face, arms flailing the air, while he thunders at
men to come to an altar and get right with God.

Plainly speaking, Bob was no longer merely the Chaplain of Bourbon Street. This was difficult even for Bob to accept for he is still better known as the Chaplain of Bourbon Street than he is as Bob Harrington. However, the man who is being used to move many people across America to Christ today is basically and predominantly a soul-winner—more specifically a winner of men.

The tag, "Chaplain of Bourbon Street" brings to mind a gregarious individual going in and out of bars in the French Quarter in New Orleans. It does not call to mind a man who can handle large crowds like no other man in America with the possible exception of Graham.

Bob likes to be known as a personal soulwinner. He sees himself as being on a perpetual manhunt for Christ. The success of every great evangelist in history has rested in his ability to multiply the concept of soulwinner and maintain a persuasive personal magnetism while preaching to the masses.

Bob's most fruitful work for the past several years has been in his crusades. In a day of dying mass evangelism and floundering group endeavors among religious institutions, Bob has been able to maintain the magic that keeps people coming back to hear a simple message delivered with power and wit.

For an evangelist, the ultimate proof is in his ability to draw the net; to get people to respond. When Bob speaks, people listen; when he stops, they move.

If this is true, then why should he waste time trying to create a church service in a bar? Why not let the television audience see him on the firing line where the people are real and the bullets are live?

As in most of our previous decision-making sessions, the conversation was not lengthy.

I said, "Bob, why don't you stop playing television and start filming your crusades?"

He replied, "O. K., you are my new television producer. How are you going to do it?"

Everyone knows how you become a television producer. You start by telling the kids on the block you are going to be a television producer—usually like your daddy—when you grow up. Then you go to college and get a degree in television production. Then you take a job in a TV station carrying coffee and watching how the big boys do it. I could have been so lucky.

In twenty-four hours, I had hired a 16 millimeter film crew. We chose this route for San Diego because securing a mobile unit for video tape was out of sight financially. The idea was simple: shoot the film on 16 millimeter; bring it back; transfer the film to tape; edit it, and you have a television program. God bless all the poor, ignorant, untrained people of the world who let a man in red tie and socks talk them into being television producers.

On their way from New Orleans to San Diego, our film crew ran off a runway on a DC 10 in Houston; showed up with insufficient film; had only one sound camera; didn't have enough light; and were mad at me because I didn't know what I was doing.

Fortunately, in San Diego, the suds were in the water and not the soap. Because, poor as our efforts were mechanically, Bob was never more powerful. And we managed to capture, not only Bob's preaching, but some unforgettable scenes during the invitation.

One film clip showed Bob sitting on the edge of the platform with his feet dangling in front of him. Over two hundred people had come forward and were crowded at his feet. He began interviewing the people. To two hippie-types he said, "People have been more concerned with your hair than your heart; more concerned about whether you were shaved than saved. But I want you to know Christ loves you."

To a black man he said, "You cannot help the way you were born black any more than I can help the way I was born white. But, we can both be glad we have been washed in the red blood of Christ."

An aged and crippled man was standing toward the back of those at the front. Bob said, "Let him through," and the group parted to make a path for him. Bob took him by the hand, leaned down and prayed that God would touch his body as well as his heart.

Now that's what people give money to see happen. And they saw it from San Diego.

This is the way Bob summed it up in his November *Heartbeat:*

CRUSADES ARE COMBINED WITH TELEVISION IN UNPRECENDENTED EFFORT TO REACH AMERICA

Please follow what I am about to say carefully. The information on this page marks the most significant turning point of my entire ministry and you have helped make it possible.

Up to this point, the two principle forms of outreach for my ministry have been crusades and television. Although both have been used greatly to reach people for Christ, I have felt that the two were going to have to work together if we are going to reach America for Christ. This dilemma has caused me many nights of soul searching.

First, let me describe my dilemma, and then let me show how God solved it.

I. *The Dilemma*

    1. In the past, I have been preaching in crusades and then returning home to tape my television programs.

    2. This has created a double preparation on my part and has not let you share directly in the crusades.

    3. Also there is a different atmosphere when you are talking to 40 or 50 invited guests and when you are preaching to thousands who need Christ.

    4. Also you have been supporting me financially in the endeavor to reach souls for Christ and you have not had the chance to see this taking place.

II. *How God Solved the Dilemma*

    1. Last month God revealed the solution to me. If the crusades are where the people are being reached for Christ, then why not film the crusades for television?

    2. This is what we have been doing this month:

        1.) Our San Diego Crusade (where 100,000 attended in eight days and over 2,000 were saved) is being shown on "Chaplain of Bourbon Street" during the four weekends of October.

        2.) Our Washington Crusade will be shown during November.

        3.) Our Los Angeles Crusade will be shown during December.

        4.) Our Fort Worth Crusade will be shown during January.

        5.) Our climactic Spiritual Bowl in Columbia, South Carolina (where over 20,000 gathered on New Year's Eve last year) will be shown during February.

    3. From now on, even those who watch television will see what God is doing in our crusades.

    4. From now on, every time I preach in our crusades, I will know that 6 million more people will hear my message every week!

Everything was good about San Diego (except the television producer.) The preaching was good; the preachers were cooperative; the people were responsive; the offering was generous.

In the ministerial vernacular, San Diego was a mountain top experience. And from that vantage point, Bob looked down on what lay immediately on the horizon. From San Diego, he boarded a plane and flew 3,000 miles across America to begin Washington—Phase II.

One man alone in Washington.

CHAPTER VIII

Why Again?
Why Not?
WASHINGTON–PHASE II

Those on Bob's mailing list in September, 1973, received this information from him about Washington—Phase II:

WASHINGTON—PHASE—II—SPECIAL!
CONSTITUTION HALL—SEPTEMBER 25-27

Why Washington?

I. *Let me mention some definite reasons why I am not going back to Washington:*
   1. I am not going to point an accusing finger.
   2. I am not going to try to "solve Watergate."
   3. I am not going to add to the burden of any citizen, senator or president.
   4. I am not going to "save our government."
II. *Rather there are certain positive factors in my choice of Washington as a continuing pulpit during the coming months.*
   1. As never before in the history of America, the eyes and ears and hearts of our entire nation are upon Washington.
      1.) I am after the eyes and ears of America.

137

2.) What I have to say is far more important than Watergate, and will still be a subject for discussion long after Watergate has passed into history.

2. I am not going to Washington to be a part of the problem, but to be a part of the solution.

1.) Every person will spend most of his time either digging up problems and questions or searching after solutions and answers.

2.) The problems we are facing in America today are moral and spiritual and are as old as man.

3.) The answers I bring in the Name of God belong to God and are as old as God's relation to man and yet as timely as today's newspapers.

3. I am going to Washington because God, for reasons I do not fully understand, has laid upon my shoulders the role of a prophet.

1.) A prophet, in the Biblical sense, does not predict rain, or when the fish will bite, or, in some magical way, foretell the future.

2.) A prophet of God rather reminds the people of his nation of the righteousness of God and calls the people to repent.

4. I am going to Washington because our nation's capitol has brought to our attention the moral stupor into which America has drifted during the past decade.

1.) And God is a God who leads people out of their dark dilemma.

2.) God didn't lead His people into the wilderness but He led them out.

3.) God didn't lead His people into captivity but He led them out.

4.) And God didn't lead America into her

present moral dilemma, but He will lead her out.

5. I am going to Washigton because God has laid it on my heart to WAKE UP AMERICA for Him in the Seventies.
   1.) I said I do not fully understand this call from God and I do not.
   2.) I have asked myself, "Why me—Bob Harrington?"
   3.) But as sure as I am alive, God, for this cause—to WAKE UP AMERICA—has brought me to this hour.
   4.) And I will not rest until, in the Seventies, in America, every eye shall see and every ear hear, and every heart feel, that It's Fun Being Saved.

6. Therefore, I am going to Washington so that I can go from there to America.
   1.) Between Washington trips I will be seeking to WAKE UP AMERICA in some part of America.
   2.) There are twenty major population centers in America.
   3.) I will have preached in each of these twenty centers during 1973.
   4.) I have already made definite plans to return to each of these 20 key areas in 1974.
   5.) Our television ministry, "Chaplain of Bourbon Street" is already being viewed in over half of these 20 population centers (we are presently on 32 stations.)
   6.) By the end of the year, we will be witnessing weekly in all these 20 key areas.

7. So I am not merely going back to Washington, but back to where the people are all across America in a prayerfully planned schedule that

God has placed on my heart.

1.) Everywhere we go, doors are opening.

2.) Everywhere we go, crowds are gathering.

3.) Everywhere we go, people are being saved.

8. Very simply put, I am going to Washington as a focal point to WAKE UP AMERICA.

   1.) Rip Van Winkle became famous because he slept 20 years.

   2.) But many have missed the significance of this old gentleman.

   3.) When he went up the hill to sleep there was a picture of King George on the village tavern.

   4.) When he came down the hill 20 years later, there was a picture of George Washington on the same tavern.

   5.) Rip didn't merely sleep 20 years. He slept through a revolution.

9. Our great nation is caught up in the greatest revolution it has ever faced.

   1.) The forces of sin and evil are seeking to destroy our finest as well as our youngest.

   2.) Watergate is only one small finger that points to our nation's moral breakdown.

   3.) The drug problem is another finger.

   4.) Rising crime is another finger.

   5.) Perverted sex is another finger.

10. And in the midst of this moral crisis, America is asleep!

    1.) And many of God's people are asleep!

    2.) And we are sleeping through a revolution!

    3.) But I will not sleep!

    4.) Nor will I let the America I love sleep in peace!

11. While there is breath within me, I will continue to take God's messages across our nation.

    1.) I will take it to the rich man's palace and

the poor man's hovel.
2. I will take it up rickety tenement steps and down to the lowest brothel.
3.) I will take it into hospitals and behind prison bars.
4.) "WAKE UP AMERICA! Jesus Saves! And It's Fun Being Saved!"

In the same *Heartbeat,* Bob had a second, more personal article about Washington:

A HEART TO HEART TALK ABOUT WASHINGTON

An Eleventh Hour Appeal

The days, hours and minutes are swiftly slipping by. Shortly, we will be on the platform in Constitution Hall, just two blocks from the White House.

Every day of late I have found myself slipping away more and more to spend time in prayer and soul searching for this next crucial venture into our nation's capitol.

Please don't mistake what I am about to say. Those who know me know I am not afraid of the devil—or anyone else! If I had been Daniel, I would have gone into the lion's den.

And yet, never have I felt a greater sense of *dependence* than at this eye of Washington—Phase II. First, dependence upon God's power and might and spirit. Second, dependence upon people like yourself who believe in what we are trying to do for Christ in our nation's capitol.

I Need You

As simply as I can say it—I NEED YOU! First, let me try to open my heart and tell you *why* I need you, and second, let me try to tell you *how I need you.*

Why I Need You

1. Washington is a big, busy lonely city. It is so easy to come and go in this great city and never be noticed. It is all but impossible for one man to come—uninvited—into this city and gain the eyes and ears, much less the hearts of the people in Capitol City.
2. *Downtown Washington is a fearful place after dark.* It would be so much easier to go to one of the beautiful churches in the cloistered hills of Virginia or Maryland than to strike at the heart of downtown in Capitol City.
3. *Constitution Hall holds 3900 people.* They told me it was a miracle that 1000 people came to the Statler Hilton each night. Now we are asking God, this trip to give us 4 times as many every night for three nights!
4. *To accomplish this, we must:*
   1.) Advertise on radio and television and in the newspapers.
   2.) Bring in personalities who love Jesus to help us.
   3.) Plan for buses to help people with transportation.
   4.) Provide for security to protect people who are willing to come.
   5.) All of this takes funds that wo do not have and are looking to God to provide.

How I Need You

1. *First, I need you to make a generous and immediate contribution to this endeavor.* Already our expenses for this trip are almost four times as much as our first trip. Every crusade I hold has a local budget and committee. We have none of that in Washington. We are on our own!

2. *Second, call on your friends to send a contribution.* You will never ask them to invest in a greater cause. No ministry is trying to strike closer to the heart of our nation's needs in this crucial hour than this one. I am not having to stand in line to schedule Constitution Hall for Christ!

3. *If you live within a day's drive of Washington, come join us!* Call our office in New Orleans. We will tell you how to arrange hotel accommodations.

4. *Call your Washington — Maryland — Virginia Christian friends and ask them to fill their church bus and join us.* We want the senators, congressmen and government people coming into Constitution Hall. It is going to be extremely difficult to bring 4,000 people into downtown Washington. I need your help!

5. *On the back side of the enclosed letter, there is a place on the coupon for your suggestions to me today!*

I am doing all I know to do; thinking all I can think; praying all I can pray; giving all I have to give. I ask your help.

Gratefully saved

Bob Harrington

Washington Phase II presented 3 basic problems: 1.) How to fill Constitution Hall's 3900 seats for three nights. 2.) How to get into higher places in government. 3.) How to get the Washington experience filmed for television.

To help boost attendance at the hall, Bob had invited some special guests to join him. Some of these cost a lot, others a little; some were black, others white; some helped, others didn't. Diplomacy prohibits being more specific about this, but it was rather unfortunate that the guests who cost Bob the most helped the least, and vice versa.

Since Washington's population is predominantly black, Bob invited the O'Neal Twins from Saint Louis, to sing for the three nights. These guys are something else; great spirits; great Christians; and can they sing gospel music!

Bob also invited Richard and Patti Roberts who appeared briefly on the second night.

The biggest hill we had to climb involved television. We had three alternatives: 1.) Try 16 millimeter again. This meant more sound cameras and more time spent in editing. 2.) Give up the remote filming idea and return to the studio. 3.) Secure a mobile TV unit and film by video tape on location.

The reason we had not gone to alternative three from the beginning was money. Every source we had checked was double what Bob was able to allot for TV production.

Then we met "The Keystone Cops!" The last day we filmed in San Diego, Jack Price and I were in his room bemoaning the television problem. Suddenly, I recalled a conversation three months earlier with Reverend Clendennen, a Pentecostal minister from Beaumont, Texas. He had told me he had a mobile TV unit that was getting too expensive for his sole use. He asked me to stay on the lookout for someone who might be interested in videoing his crusades.

I had completely dismissed the conversation because, at the time, I had not "decided" to pursue the career of a television producer.

I mentioned this experience to Jack, and he said, "Call him now and see what his prices are."

I located Reverend Clendennen and told him what we needed. Within an hour, his son, Larry, called me and told me what they could do and what the cost would be.

It was a dream come true. They had video cameras, technicians, engineers, lights, a generator, and everything else! And at prices that would be less expensive than anything Bob had paid before—even in the studio!

Why do I call them the Keystone Cops? Well, for those of you who are too young to understand, I am not going to explain. To this point, "The Keystoners" themselves do not know the etymology of this tag and I don't plan to tell them. I think some of you may guess in the next couple of pages. I want to say now that nothing in this presentation is meant to cast a bad reflection on those Pentecostal boys from Beaumont. They may have rented the wrong size generator at Washington, and they may have mistakenly driven to San Francisco instead of Los Angeles—but no group of kids ever worked harder and loved God more while they did it. You will read their worst in the next few pages. However, at this writing, the Keystoners have turned out some of the most beautiful TV programs Bob has ever had.

Jack and I arrived in Washington ahead of Bob to make sure that everything was in order. We needed a grand piano for the O'Neal Twins. It had arrived. We needed the O'Neal Twins. They had arrived. The Keystoners were to arrive for the first night and get set up. Then they were to film the next two nights. We received a call that they had broken down in Atlanta, Georgia and would not be in until the next day.

We had flooded radio and TV with announcements of the crusades. We had made special mailings and put up billboards. Now the time had come. Together with the O'Neal Twins, Bob, Jack and I made our way to Constitution Hall to face the music.

If we had been at the Statler Ballroom, we would have

Bob and C. A. Roberts inside the mobile unit of the top brass of Bob's television crew. (Left to Right) Paul Lee, engineer, C. A., Robert Turnage, director, and Bob.

had a standing room only crowd. However, on that first night in Constitution Hall, we had 1200 people literally rattling around in an ocean of empty seats.

I think if Bob were to allow himself a moment of complete honesty, he would admit that on that night, it really wasn't fun being saved.

It was a terribly disappointing experience. We returned to the hotel and tried to rationalize the matter over a late dinner. No luck. Jack and I had flown all night from the West Coast and were tired. Bob had circled by Cleveland and appeared on a talk show en route. Bob's words at the dinner table were certainly understandable under the circumstances.

"This is not Las Vegas," he said. "There are enough preachers alone in the Washington, Maryland, Virginia area to fill that hall. And there are religious organizations around here by the bushel basket. And they know we need support. What, under God, do they think we are trying to do? I have written them all and begged them to help. Where are they?"

If any of them can give me an adequate answer to that question, I wish they would send it to C. A. Roberts, Houston, Texas. Oh, some blacks thought the crusade should be more black; and some liberals thought it should be more liberal; and some conservatives thought it should be more conservative; and some organizations thought it

C. A. Roberts, Bob, and Ralph Daughrity, one of "The Keystoners."

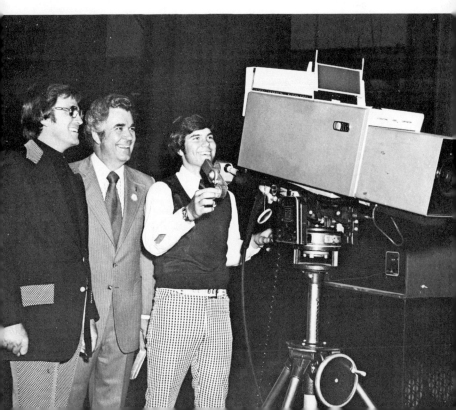

should be more organized; and some evangelicals thought it should be more evangelistic.

Such is the misfortune of institutional religion that it is shot through with self-interest, pride, indifference and hypocrisy. The truth was that no one, including God himself, had a right to come uninvited, into another's territory.

Bob was simply too religious to attract the average sinner of Washington, sight unseen, and too unorthodox to attract the average Washington religionist. The result was that he was left to sink or swim with a thousand or so people who cared in the city the whole world was watching.

I figured the one truly good thing that could emanate from this Washington trip would be the television. Many people across the country had responded to Bob's appeal to help him go to Washington—both trips. These people needed to *see* Bob in action in Washington.

Since the inside of Constitution Hall isn't automatically identifiable with Washington, and because we thought it would be more in keeping with Bob's style, we wanted to do one program outside.

We agreed on the Lincoln Memorial.

Wednesday morning I made some inquiries and found we would need a permit for the Memorial filming. I made an appointment to be at the Parks office at 1:00 PM. The Keystoners were to arrive at noon and I was going to get them started at the Hall. They had trouble finding Constitution Hall and did not arrive until after 1:00 o'clock. So far, no real problem. The people at the Parks office rescheduled me for 3:30 PM.

Our TV boys took a close look at the Hall. Their immediate observations were: 1.) They did not bring enough cable. 2.) They did not have enough lights. This is like a

Bob preaching in Constitution Hall in Washington (Phase II).

sick person who is improving except for two things: (1.) His heart isn't beating. (2.) He isn't breathing.

We now knew, before we began, that the cameras would have to be much closer to Bob than we had hoped; and that, regardless of how close they were, we still were not going to have sufficient light to make sharp programs. Light is 90% of the battle.

I told the boys to go to work and get it as good as they could. I mentioned to them that I had to leave to go get permission for the filming outside at Lincoln Memorial.

At this point, the other boot hit the floor. The boys began to explain to me that they did not, in fact, have a generator. They were planning to buy one, but had not done so yet.

"But you told me," I said to Robert Turnage, the director, "that you would have a generator here in Washington so we could film outside."

"I know, Brother Roberts, and we planned to do just that. We got a preacher friend over here in Virginia who's got a generator."

"Good," I said, feeling like I didn't mean it, "then you can have a generator at Lincoln Memorial in the morning."

"Well, Brother Roberts, I don't know about tomorrow. Our friends said we could use his generator Tuesday or Wednesday, but he didn't say anything about Thursday."

"Robert, you weren't here Tuesday, and this is Wednesday!" I now knew things weren't good. "Tomorrow is the last day we will be here."

"Brother Roberts, don't you worry; we will find a generator somewhere in this town."

"Good." I said it again, still not believing.

I made my way over to the Bureau of Parks. I was prepared to fight my way through a maze of red tape. I wish I could remember the woman's name. There was a lot of detail—several agencies had to be contacted; the group cleaning the Memorial had to give clearance; the police needed to approve. Several key officials had to be called to see if any other use was being made of the Memorial. A sheet of information had to be given about Bob. All of this—calls, information—was completed by this one extremely charming woman in less than 15 minutes.

I met Bob and Jack back at the hotel for an early dinner. I decided that I would not share with Bob any of the problems regarding the televising. At this point, my producer instinct told me everything was going to work out O. K.

Bob was on cloud nine—or seventh heaven, if you prefer. He had a spent a major portion of his morning with Melvin Laird (who at this writing is Advisor to the President) in his White House Office. Mr. Laird had been a fan of Bob's for several years.

Bob had gone by that morning to see his barber friend, Jack Allen. Jack has a regular shop in the Capitol. Each Wednesday he goes to his shop in the White House. When

Senator Vinegar Bend Mizell giving his testimony at Constitution Hall, Washington (Phase II).

Bob entered the shop, Jack immediately said, "Would you like to see Mr. Laird?" Before Bob could reply, he continued, "He would like to visit with you."

Melvin Laird is a very sincere and devout man. While he was Secretary of Defense, he opened a chapel in the Pentagon, which was later dedicated to him. It was in this chapel Bob had spoken on his first trip to Washington.

The Chaplain and the Presidential Advisor spent a considerable period of time in serious discussion. Finally, Mr. Laird asked Bob to lead them in prayer before he left. The two of them sat side by side on the sofa, with hands clasped together, and prayed for their nation.

As Bob left, Mr. Laird pledged his support to any future efforts to witness for Christ in Washington. This was the closest to the center Bob had reached. It boosted his

Bob preaching inside the Pentagon. Two hundred men come to the altar to pray.

Bob receiving military escort for his message at the Pentagon (Phase II).

spirits and would prove far more significant to Bob's witness in government in the future.

The second night crowd showed little change in size. This left Bob staring at the wide circle of upper-level empty seats. I tried to encourage him by reminding him how many millions of people would see and hear his actions that night. Somebody should have been encouraging me. This was my first time ever to work with a mobile TV unit.

I needed every advantage. Instead, everything was bad; poor camera placement and faulty lighting were only part of the problem. Richard and Patti Roberts were appearing on this night, and it was necessary for us to shut the cameras down during their part to insure them we would not bootleg them onto a later program of Bob's.

We made it through the night—but everything was flat. Fortunately, when Bob is bad, he is far above average. But the size of the crowd took away whatever lift Mr. Laird had given him. We were all too tired, and too dejected to eat that night. We were supposed to be at Lincoln Memorial at 9:00 AM to film. The Keystoners were to be there at 8:00 AM to warm up the equipment. It was necessary for us to stay with our schedule since Bob had an engagement at the Pentagon at noon.

The Keystoners called me at 8:00 the next morning to tell me they couldn't get the generator they were renting until 11:00 o'clock. This meant they would be ready to begin when Bob was supposed to be at the Pentagon.

Our only alternative was to delay the Lincoln taping until 3:00 PM. Many factors were working against this plan. The sun would be in its right place but wrong for us. Rain was predicted for the afternoon and the boys couldn't bring their equipment out if there was even a chance of rain. Also this would leave the boys too little time to reassemble both cameras for the evening service, and we would have to go with just one camera. The only factor we had in our favor was that we had no other choice.

Bob did not know what to expect at the Pentagon. Two months before, he was taken to a small chapel in one of the side corridors to speak to about twenty people. When we arrived, a large security guard was waiting for us. We were taken to the center of the main concourse.

One who has not seen this sight cannot imagine the setting. The Pentagon is a city within itself. The main concourse is complete with drugstores, grocery stores, department stores, restaurants, a Post Office, and even a large bank.

The area that had been prepared for Bob was not a room, but an open air chapel set up at the open end of the concourse. Several hundred chairs were set up in front of a piano, an organ and a pulpit. By the time Bob began to speak, not only were all the chairs filled, but hundreds of other persons were standing in the rear. When Bob gave the invitation, over 200 men came and knelt at the altar. One man said he had never seen so much big brass gathered openly in the Pentagon, much less on their knees.

This was not only the most impressive, but possibly the most significant moment of Washington—Phase II. This type thing just didn't happen in high government, much less high military. Bob showed it could be done; I mean men in high places humbling themselves openly before God and each other.

This was the whole point of Bob's trip. Why shouldn't this take place—and here? Why shouldn't revival be needed, wanted and accepted by those who were directing our government?

Maybe this was the one essential ingredient missing from modern government that was keeping the whole thing out of focus and subject to baser influences. After all, as Bob kept saying, this is a nation under God.

The men who put together our Constitution did so with a reverence for and dependence upon God. Our Republic had been born and bred in prayer, just as it had been conceived in liberty, and with justice for all. Why is it that the One our forefathers turned to first should be the One our present fathers turn to last?

It looked as if Bob was a one man show, because, at that moment he was. But he did not relish his singularity. In fact, he has now said he will not return to Washington until 100 men of God go with him. Does he mean ministers? It doesn't matter. What matters to Bob is that men of God—real men—will go and unashamedly call our nation's leaders to God.

There will be no justification for a lack of revival in Congress, the Senate, the Administration—except the indifference and lack of effort on the part of God's people. Don't try to tell Bob that our leaders are too busy or too important. He knelt with those 200 and heard their fervent

Abe listens as Bob preaches at the Lincoln Memorial.

prayers. The only missing link is concerned men of God who, like Bob, will dare entrance in the name of Christ.

When we arrived at Lincoln Memorial, our boys were apparently ready. The sun was out—not a cloud in the sky. Bob sat on the steps with a man who looks like Lincoln (and was dressed like Lincoln), the O'Neal Twins and Jack Price. He talked about truth—the kind that makes all men, of every color, free. Jack sang "The Battle Hymn of the Republic," one of his finest performances ever.

Bob, Abe, and the O'Neal twins listen as Jack sings from the steps of the Lincoln Memorial (Phase II).

Bob took his cue from a line in the Declaration of Independence: "We hold these truths to be self evident." He drove home the point that truth is not self evident. The "truth" of the Declaration was true for those who wrote it for they were living through it. But every generation has to rediscover truth for itself. He had come to Washington to lead in a rediscovery that the truth of Jesus Christ can set men free.

Bob and Abe on the steps of the Lincoln Memorial (Phase II).

It was a truly beautiful and historic moment. Tragically enough, all of our mechanics would prove faulty. We would learn later that The Keystoners had rented a generator with the wrong time-base frequency. Despite everything we did later to alter the problem, we were left with tape that had "video noise", which was below broadcast quality. Since we also filmed the opening and closing of the other three programs from Lincoln Memorial, we were left with four faulty programs.

Television stations later refused to air the programs. Bob wrote all his stations explaining the historic nature of the programs. Every station except one cooperated and aired the Washington programs.

It was embarassing for Bob to be identified with such poor TV quality. How the TV producer kept from being fired I'll never know—except that Bob's mail response to the poor Washington programs was his best ever to that time.

I recall something my coach friend, Bill Peterson, said when he was coach at Florida State University. He had just beaten Mississippi Southern. I asked him what he thought of the game. He replied, "We looked bad and won. Last week we looked good and lost. I would rather look bad and win." In Washington, Bob looked bad and won. Why? Because the people who support ministries such as his are not as concerned with video noise and poor lighting as they are whether a man is trying to stand in the gap for Jesus Christ.

CHAPTER IX

"Victory has a thousand fathers; defeat is an orphan."

John F. Kennedy

LOS ANGELES

There will be no intention, in this chapter, to fix blame on any person. Those who probably should receive blame slipped, early enough, into nameless oblivion. Those who are mentioned by name at least stayed to the end and did what they could to help in ways each thought best. If anyone should accept blame for Bob's crusade in Los Angeles, it would have to be the person, or persons, who first conceived the idea, "Key 73."

Key 73 was a concept that foresaw the possibility of churches of all denominations cooperating in an endeavor to work together in the name of evangelism. The idea of churches working together on anything is contingent upon ministers being able to deliver their people to whatever they—the ministers—commit their churches to.

The idea may have worked back in the days when party bosses controlled precincts and ministers controlled congregations. But ours is a day of deteriorating authority on the part of the local minister. A decade ago, when a minister said, "Count on my church," you could count on the participation of a majority of his active constituents. Today, when a minister says this, he means, "I will try to be there myself." Most ministers simply can no longer deliver their people.

Why the ministers' authority has diminished is not the subject of this chapter. The consequence of this fact, however, is basically what made the Los Angeles Key 73 Crusade a farce from beginning to end.

I was in Bob's office in New Orleans in late 1972, along with Jack Price and Max Morris, when Bob received the initial call from Dr. Harold Fickett, minister of the First Baptist Church, Van Nuys, California, inviting him to be the speaker for the Los Angeles Key 73 Crusade, October 21–28, 1973. He mentioned there were over 3400 churches in the greater Los Angeles area and that above 700 of them could probably be counted on to cooperate in the crusade.

During the early conversations between Bob and the L. A. people, which were a year in advance of the crusade, every indication Bob was getting was that they—the Key 73 Committee—expected this to be possibly the largest effort on the West Coast in years. In fact, they wanted to have two crusades going simultaneously—one in the southern area and one in the north—with possibly a single climactic service in the Hollywood Bowl. They wanted to use a black as the second preacher, and have the two men alternate each night between crusades.

Bob expressed the problem this presented to him. In order to operate his ministry soundly, he used the same formula in all his crusades: 1.) agree with the local people on a budget 2.) the local people would try to raise as much of the budget in advance by gifts from participating churches 3.) the offerings from the first 4 nights of the crusade would be used to defray crusade expenses 4.) the offering the last 4 nights would go to the Bob Harrington Ministry.

A plan such as this, in substance, is standard procedure whenever a local group invites an outside evangelist. If the local group did not have certain nights for raising the budget, they could be left in a hole. If, however, the visiting evangelist were to agree to take whatever is left after the expenses are raised, he could be left in an even bigger hole. He would be left at the mercy of one or all of several bad alternatives: 1.) the local people might overspend the budget 2.) they might be lax in raising funds in advance of the meeting 3.) they could, therefore, go through the final service with the budget still unmet, leaving the evangelist with nothing.

Often the local groups will agree to raise all funds in advance. This is an evangelist's dream. Sometimes they ask only for the first couple of services to offset budget expenses. Rarely will a group ask for more services to go to the budget than are left for the evangelist. However, the local group should have the prerogative to set any plan they choose—since it is their crusade, *so long as they notify the evangelist in advance.* If, then, he feels he cannot comply with their conditions, he can always choose not to come.

Let me digress to explain that not all evangelistic organizations function alike. Some are completely subsidized from outside sources. Some are sufficiently funded from outside sources so that they plan to lose money in crusades. Bob's ministry is set up so that he has to count crusades as a revenue source.

Bob has two parts to his ministry—crusades and television. The latter, television, presently spends four dollars for every one dollar it brings in. It is a hungry, growing child. It could be years before television stands on its own two feet.

He has four basic sources of income for his ministry: crusades, television, books and records and mail response. His mail ministry is almost as young in development as television. The sale of books and records offsets the overhead for his staff and Bourbon Street ministry. This leaves Bob only one source for the funding of his television outreach: crusades.

This does not mean that Bob always counts on making money from a crusade. Often he plans to invest in the crusade ministry, as in Washington. He could have no sanity to his ministry if he could not plan ahead and project where he would gain and where he would lose.

Unfortunately, he was led to believe that Los Angeles would be a plus to his ministry financially. It was his understanding that the Key 73 committee both understood and accepted his terms of four nights for them and four for him on the offering. I must stress that it was his understanding because, again unfortunately, some of these agreements were made in good faith by phone, and with persons who were no longer even a part of the crusade by the time it took place.

In June of 1973, Bob received a letter from Reverend Dale Scott, an associate minister at The First Baptist Church, Van Nuys. It was not understood at the time whether Reverend Scott had actually become the crusade chairman or whether he was simply assisting Dr. Fickett in his responsibilities for Key 73. There were certain warning signs in the letter that Bob, in retrospect, should have taken more seriously. The letter was as follows:

June 19, 1973

Dear Bob

Thanks for your letter regarding our Los Angeles Crusade in October 21–28. Dr. Fickett, and the "Key '73" committee are hard at work in planning and promoting the crusade.

The Shrine Auditorium holds 6,500. The choir will accommodate 300 and still leave us room back stage to do personal work for those who make decisions.

The money for "Key '73" Crusade will have to be taken during our meetings basicly (sic). We are working on many churches to (make) some kind of advance gifts.

We know that the Holy Spirit will reward God's Word as you preach and Jack sings. This is the way that Christ is fully honored as people repent and come to Jesus and invite Him into their hearts.

We have Campus Crusade doing the Counseling Training and they will do the Follow-up work. You might write to:

Mr. Henry Schneider
Campus Crusade for Christ International
1738 North Waterman Ave., Suite #4
San Bernardino, California 92404

and give him an idea what your style of invitation will be. As I see it in the Shrine Auditorium, there is not an awful lot of room up front, but God will provide.

Keep praying for us here and we all are praying for your ministry. We shall rejoice in what God hath done for Los Angeles. I remain in Christ's service.

Yours

Rev. Dale M. Scott, Director
Special Ministries Department

By this time, the Key 73 group had evidently settled on one crusade and one evangelist. The note Bob should have picked up on related to the crusade expenses. At this time, he did not interpret the third paragraph to imply that he would be held responsible for all the expenses of the crusade. He made a phone call for clarification and attached a memo to the letter, indicating the points he made. They were:

1. Who is the Chairman of Key 73?

2. What are the financial conditions of the last 5 nights of crusade?

3. We are not responsible for Key 73 debts.

Unknown to Bob, during the summer months, Key 73 in Los Angeles began falling apart. There were many factors involved. A television production incurred heavy debts. The Chairman of Key 73 pulled out for personal reasons. There were other problems which are not pertinent to this writing. The point is that all this was greatly affecting the status of the crusade in October and was, as yet, unknown to Bob.

Any man knows he can make the decision to be for or against his marriage as he chooses. If a man wants to think of good things about his wife, he can find many. Conversely, if he wants to list bad things, he can find legion. The choice is his. Similarly, if ministers want to find reasons for supporting a crusade, they can do it. If they want to find reasons for not supporting a crusade, this is a very simple exercise to achieve.

Bob spoke for a National Religious Broadcasters meeting in September at the Church of the Open Door in Los Angeles. This was one of those cases of Bob doing a favor for someone, at a real inconvenience to himself (as a result, he had to fly all night to his next engagement) and drew nothing but ill will from it. First, he did not realize that a number came that night to find fault. Second, he did not realize that the ministers of Los Angeles were already looking for reasons not to support the Key 73 Crusade.

At the conclusion of the NRB meeting, Bob gave an invitation. Many people began to leave. Bob scolded the people for leaving. The next week two psychiatrists who had attended sent letters to the Church of the Open Door saying they were convinced that Bob's outburst was the product of a demented mind! Sponsors of the meeting gave a different interpretation. They said that the ones leaving literally blocked the aisles, rendering it impossible for those making decisions to reach the front! It was a case where each person drew the response from the meeting that he chose to make.

Three weeks before time for the L. A. Crusade, I received a call from Dr. Harold Fickett, who is a close friend of mine and also Bob's. He said, "C. A., I have tried to reach Bob. You have to get word to him that this Los Angeles Crusade is collapsing."

I asked him the reason. He replied, "The ministers are all for Bob; they just don't want to go downtown to the Shrine Auditorium. They feel it is dangerous and out of the way."

I said, "Are you pulling out, also?"

"No, I am not. Bob knows I am for him and will do what I can. I just think Bob needs to know he is going to have a battle here."

As I relayed the conversation to Bob, we did not know what to make of it. Why bring up Shrine Auditorium at this time? They had scheduled it, not Bob, over six months before, and had actually signed a contract for the auditorium. Also, Bob had spoken two weeks earlier, to 160 ministers from the area, and received no such negative response.

In retrospect, someone representing Key 73 should have sent Bob a letter cancelling Key 73's part in the crusade. The only inference is that this was not done either because by this time no one was in charge, or because they did not know what their liability was regarding their contract with Shrine Auditorium, which was for a minimum commitment of $8,000.

In all fairness to Dr. Fickett, it must be said that he was doing everything he could to solve the problem which he saw as very real at the time. It had not been "his" crusade to begin with, nor was it his to cancel.

From Bob's perspective, he was committed, at this late stage, to a point of no return. He had personally invested several thousand dollars for a mass mailing to the L. A. area, announcing the crusade, that had already been mailed. Also, in anticipation of a good week for his ministry, he had already invested over five thousand dollars to bring a mobile TV unit to L. A. to film "Chaplain of Bourbon Street." Per his agreement, with the TV people, he would not only be out the money by cancelling this late, but would have to make other plans for December programs at twice the cost!

When all else fails, you punt! Bob chose to send a second emergency letter to those on his mailing list. This was the substance of the letter:

October 4, 1973

Dear Joann

Since I have nowhere to turn, I must come to you with a burden that is heavy on my heart. When you

read this, I will be preaching in Shrine Auditorium in
Los Angeles—October 21–28. Today, October 2, I
received a call from the chairman of the Los Angeles
crusade. He was very downhearted.

He said all the preachers were for me, but they were
afraid. They were afraid the people wouldn't come
downtown to Shrine Auditorium. They were afraid
they would not be able to raise the budget. I could
tell they wanted me to say, "Let's wait until another
time." That isn't what I said.

I said we will never reach America through little
faith. I said that I would come, the people will come;
and the bills will be paid.

The first service in Shrine Auditorium was Sunday afternoon. I arrived in L. A. on Monday. I have never seen
Bob so low. The Shrine seats 6,500. There had been 1,000
present Sunday. The Shrine people had thrown in insur-
ance, security, ushers, stage hands, raising the cost from
$8,000 to $14,000. There was no Key 73! Reverend Dale
Scott, who had personally borrowed $2,000 to cover pub-
licity, was still in the boat, as was Dr. Fickett. Bob had
called his office to stop the Keystoners from leaving. They
were already enroute.

We discussed the alternatives. At this stage, it was not
Bob's baby; Key 73 that is. He could turn the TV boys
back in Tucson, Arizona and have them film Fort Worth
for December. This would give us time to decide where
to go from there for January—for which Fort Worth was
already scheduled, TV-wise. The losses Bob would have
by pulling out would be small in comparison to what he
would have if he stayed.

I called Dr. Fickett to see if he would move the crusade to his church. He said we could if we would pay
$150 per night for lights.

Having been the pastor of a large church, I felt this was unnecessary, but you don't look a gift horse in the mouth. Besides, Harold could have hid behind "his board" and abstained. Instead, he made it possible for us to proceed.

At this point, I became the middle man for a hopeless situation. Bob was telling me he was counting on me to make clear to the right people that he would not be responsible for Key 73 bills and he still expected to get the last four nights offering for his ministry. Dr. Fickett was telling me that, in moving the meeting to his church, he was not going to assume the financial responsibility for the crusade.

Everyone was looking after his own interest. Mine was television. I was convinced that the only good thing that might come from this orphan crusade would be some good television programs. I told Bob I would do what I could and I told Dr. Fickett the same. I crossed my fingers and told the Keystoners to keep coming.

The services for the remainder of the week, in First Baptist, Van Nuys, were some of the most powerful I have ever witnessed. By Thursday night, the bills for the total crusade had not been reached. Bob consented to let the night's offering go to the crusade. As it turned out later, this was a formality on his part, for it was beyond his control.

The offerings for Friday night, Saturday night and Sunday afternoon also went to the crusade. Unfortunately, Dr. Fickett began announcing on Friday night that the offering was going to Bob. This later created a lot of resentment on the part of people who would not have given to an expense offering, but did wish to give to Bob.

Dr. Fickett, in fact, had not misrepresented things. The offering, in theory, was going to Bob. The only change, which had never been defined by anyone, was that the entire Los Angeles Key 73 Crusade had become Bob's responsibility.

There should be a forum for negotiating such circumstances. Bob deserved a court of last resort where he could say, "Look! I didn't invite myself here. I could have left Monday and someone would have been out on a limb for thousands of dollars. Dale Scott would have to eat a two thousand dollar loan. Let's split the difference. I'll bear half and those who first thought this fiasco up bear the other half." There was no such forum.

Finally, on the last night, this announcement was made to the packed house. "To this point, all the money received has gone to pay Key 73 bills. But tonight, every penny you give will go to Bob."

At the end of the service, I was trying to get the Keystoners out of town (actually their truck blew up that night and they couldn't leave for a week) when I passed Bob, who was talking to the treasurer for Key 73. The man informed him that there were still a few hundred dollars of unpaid Key 73 bills, and those in charge were under orders not to give Bob any offering until all bills were paid. The problem was compounded by the fact that Dr. Fickett had to leave town and was not present to reconcile the dilemma.

Several weeks later, the Key 73 Committee did send Bob a check. In the same mail, he also received additional bills for advertising during the crusade.

And so ended another chapter in the highs and lows of Bob Harrington. Dale Scott did a good job. Dr. Harold Fickett went beyond the call of duty. Bob gave his best. The culprit was Key 73, a sickly testimony to the sterility of organized religion in this decade.

At this writing the television which emanated from Los

Angeles appears to be the best Bob has ever sent across the nation.

Those who watched Bob's program during December saw one service which reminded me of what I have read about the response to the preaching of Francis of Assissi. He used to go from village to village preaching repentance with such power that the people would rise up and say, "We will leave our jobs; we will starve; we will die; but we must serve Jesus."

On the Friday night service in L. A., Bob preached on repentance. At the conclusion of the sermon, he did not have the people stand or even bow their heads. There was no music. He called for people to come in open repentance. Hundreds began filling the aisles; the stairs leading down to the front from the balcony were filled. It was a moving testimony to the power of God at work.

Let me now put Los Angeles in perspective from Bob's vantage point. As of this writing, Los Angeles is two month's history. I have dwelt very heavily on the problems in general, and money in particular. The other day I overheard Bob describing the Los Angeles Crusade to someone. These were his words:

"God really blessed us in L. A. We had powerful invitations. Hundreds were saved. God did a wonderful thing in that crusade. I'm just glad he let me be a part of it."

He did not utter one negative word. To hear him tell, there was nothing but victory for the Lord in L. A., at least that's all that was important to him.

David said something in the 23rd Psalm about the fact that only goodness and mercy had followed him all his days. Now we know David had experienced a lot that was neither good nor merciful. But I suppose that David was so grateful for the good things of God, and committed to the advancement of God's grace and mercy, that he had chosen to see nothing else. At least, for him, there was so much good that it literally crowded out the bad.

There were 439 people saved in Los Angeles. Because of television, the nation will share in these spiritual victories. And, for Bob, that is goodness and mercy. He chooses, in retrospect, to see nothing else. This attitude is what makes him worthy of his calling.

CHAPTER X

Come Apart and Rest or Come Apart
BOB IN RETREAT

There is a paradox regarding Bob's attitude toward other preachers which, in fairness both to him and them, deserves clarification. Bob knows that his ministry is stronger when ministers support him, but he will also, on occasion, make the statement, often publicly, that he doesn't need the help of preachers.

The tragic error that repeatedly occurs in communication is that a person will say something, meaning one thing by it, and the hearer places a completely different meaning on what he heard. In cases such as this, the burden rests on the speaker. It is his responsibility to be as clear as possible regarding what he *means* by what he *says*.

Why would Bob ever say he doesn't need the preachers and what does he mean by it? Every time I have heard Bob say this, it has been in the same context. Bob has a firm conviction about the nature of his crusades. He is convinced that he must be able to control where he goes for crusades and when. In the great majority of instances, Bob schedules his own crusades. He will determine that he should go to a particular city. He will call and secure a place—usually a civic auditorium or a coliseum—and then check with some local ministers for assistance in the crusade.

This approach is almost essential if Bob wants to culti-vate his television ministry. One of the principal factors that contributes to the growth of the viewing audience is a personal appearance in that area. Earlier in the year, when we cut some stations, we found that Bob's response was weakened in areas where he had not held a crusade.

If he left this situation to the invitation from local peo-ple, years could go by before he would get into some cru-cial areas of the country. From Bob's perspective, he neither has the time nor the funding to leave his sched-uling at the mercy of others.

This approach does not ingratiate Bob to local min-isters. They have their own scheduling problems. There are things going on in their churches that, for them, have top priority. They resent an outside evangelist coming into their city with no regard for their schedules, and then presuming that they should be willing to drop their plans and support his.

Hence, the dilemma. Bob decides to go into "Anycity, U.S.A." He then asks a group of ministers to meet with him and plan the crusade. The anycity preachers meet with him and explain that the time is not right and they will not be able to support the crusade. At this point, Bob says that he understands their problem. Then he proceeds to say that he doesn't need them. What he *means* is that, with sufficient publicity, he will still be able to get a good crowd for his crusade. Bob means no harm by the state-ment. To him, he is simply telling the truth.

Jack Price and I have contended with Bob, and Bob has conceded, that he does not *need* to make such a state-ment. If he feels he must go into a city, he can do so with-out isolating the local ministers unnecessarily.

Bob is not unwise in seeing the value of local church participation. He knows any given crusade will be better to the extent that he has local help.

The problem, as I see it, goes much deeper than this. Bob once considered starting a program to put ideas regarding motivation and inspiration into the hands of fellow ministers. The project didn't get off the ground because, as Bob said, "Those ministers who want my help are sharp enough not to need it, and those who need it, don't want it."

What we have here appears to be a problem of jealousy; but it is more. Ministers, especially those of a more conservative trend, often have difficulty being compassionate and redemptive with each other. They will often spend more time trying to see through each other, instead of trying to see each other through. This is not Bob speaking, but myself. At a certain stage in my own ministry, I suffered greatly at the hands of a few ministers.

I must also add that I was helped immensely by a few ministers. The same has been true for Bob. He has been criticised harshly and unnecessarily by some preachers. But he has also been criticized by those who love him and sincerely want to help his ministry.

The problem is, how does one tell which is which? Bob has settled on a solution which I believe is both healthy and constructive. He takes everything that any minister says about him or his ministry very seriously. In fact, this type thinking led Bob to finish 1973 with a deep personal soul searching experience just as he had begun the year with a similar experience in Washington.

As the year drew to a close, Bob's heart was very heavy. He indicated to Jack that he wanted to clear the schedule and get away awhile to study and pray. He asked Jack to come with him. A friend loaned Bob a beachhouse out on the West Coast. I went out for part of the time.

We sat one evening by an open fire. Bob had been in a season of study and prayer. He was not depressed, but was in a very serious mood.

"This ministry must be the kind God can use for His purposes to reach America. I know America is either going to have revival or one big collective nervous breakdown. I want to be the minister God can use. And this means I must be the man God wants me to be. If there is an undisciplined bone in my body, or undedicated motive in my heart, I am going to change, with God's help, before I leave this place."

As I sat there I had the strong feeling that people needed to see the heart of this man. I asked Bob to let me bring the TV crew to the beach. I told him he didn't have to make a big fanfare. He and Jack could just sit out in the sand and have a prayer meeting.

Later in the week, we did just that. On the weekend of December 30, people saw a beautiful sight on TV. Bob walked the beach in meditation as he had done often during those days. He and Jack sat on the beach with an open Bible and prayed for God to fill them and lead them.

When time came to leave his retreat, Bob was a revived man. He had been back to Bethel. He had taken both himself and his ministry as seriously as he knew how. As he left, he said, "1973 has been a good year. Because of TV, I have reached more people this year than all the previous 14 years combined. But we have just scratched the surface.

"I know God has something big for me to do in 1974. I do not know yet what it is. But I know I am ready."

Several weeks later, while Bob was with Rex Humbard at the Cathedral of Tomorrow, Rex made a suggestion to Bob regarding 1974, and Bob said, "That's it!"

CHAPTER XI

Every Eye Shall See
Every Ear Shall Hear
BOB THE CIRCUIT RIDER

Rex Humbard is a good man for Bob to be around. Rex has known his share of adversity, and come through it a better man. And he really is a good man. Rex Humbard won me during a conversation he had with Bob while Bob was preaching for him Thanksgiving week.

Bob related to Rex how difficult it was for him to rise above attacks that were made on him personally or on his ministry. Rex looked at him and said this:

"Bob, all you have to do is stay with the Lord, and I will stay with you. I have had people come to me and tell me I shouldn't use you. They didn't like something you said, or something they heard you did." I told them they were wrong. I said, 'if Bob is innocent, we should stand by him. If he is guilty of a mistake, I believe he has repented. If he hasn't, I will help him repent. Bob loves God and I love Bob; and we in Christian work need Bob's voice. Let's stand by him.'"

Before Rex said this, Bob had already told me he wanted this book dedicated to Rex. After the conversation, I understood why.

During that same conversation, Rex said, "Bob, a few years ago, I made a suggestion to Oral (Roberts). I told him there were 66 population' centers in the country. If he would plan 66 crusades, three days each in length, he could cover America in one year! Oral chose not to do it, but I still think it's a good idea."

Bob knew that very moment that he was the one for the job. Later, during a midnight dinner, he couldn't stop talking about it.

"This is exactly in keeping with what God has already laid on my heart about every eye seeing, and every ear hearing and every heart feeling that It's Fun Being Saved. The thing I don't want to happen is for TV to make a remote impersonal preacher out of me. Sure, I hope someday I can reach America through television. But I want to see America being saved; and hear America being saved. And I want people to know I care."

Of course, Rex's idea wasn't as easy as it sounded. In fact, it just may not be either practical or possible; and maybe that's why "Big O" (as Rex calls Oral Roberts) didn't do it.

We retired to Bob's room and discussed the project for several hours into the night. As we entered the room Bob found a piece of paper and began drawing the picture of a bus. On the side of the bus he printed, "Bob The Circuit Rider." Jack took a pillow and laid on his side across the bed.

"You aren't planning to ride that bus are you?"

Bob smiled at Jack, "Yes, and so are you. We won't have any choice. We will be having two crusades a week instead of two a month. We will be closing one night in one town and beginning the next night in the next town.

"Even if we could make it by air, we would be spending

what little time we have for rest and study going to and from airports."

Jack sat up, his eyes reflecting excitement. "Not only that, but if we could make it, our sound equipment and books and records couldn't. This way we could climb on the bus, with all our supplies and equipment, and go to sleep. By the time we awoke, we would be at our next stop."

"That's what I mean by Circuit Rider," Bob continued as he began pacing the floor. "There is something about this that sounds like things used to be in America. Instead of a horse and a saddle pack, we'll have a bus. People will know our itinerary. They will know to be watching for us."

"And, if we wanted to," Jack was now on his feet, "we could stop in a town and have a street service and then keep on moving!"

"I mean," Bob picked it up again, "we will live on that bus! We'll fix it so we can eat on it and sleep on it; we'll put a bathroom on it. We won't have to worry about whether our books and records will arrive, or our sound. We'll all go together. Actually, this will be less expensive than air travel."

"You realize," I injected, "that this means cancelling your 1974 schedule and creating a new schedule that will add forty new crusades and follow an itinerary that will not be prohibitive for the busdriver to make in one day."

Bob sat on the bedside, "Yea, how are we going to do that?"

Jack responded: "I think we will need some time, maybe a few months, to get things prepared. It will take some time to get a bus and get it ready. Also, we owe it to the people who are expecting us during the next few months to stay with the plans they have made. Some of these have already spent money in preparation."

"Sure," Bob added, "and we will do everything we can to stay with our present commitments and fill in around them."

"Also," I said, "I think you need to give people a little time—at least several months—to let sink in just what you are doing. I mean this all sounds good sitting here. But you are talking about a marathon! You have never in your life undertaken anything this demanding; maybe no minister ever has. I don't know. But I know that, if you do this, and if people get caught up in helping you, it could be the most exciting thing to happen in our highly technological, mechanical and impersonal age. I mean, this whole idea is so American!"

"Yea," Bob was on his feet again, "we could have some old-fashioned dinner-on-the-grounds."

"And," Jack added, "some old time singings."

"Let's pray," Bob said, "and thank the Lord for giving us a new lease on 1974 for Him. Dear Lord, we thank you for this night. Help us to help you. Help us to do more for you in 1974. Bless our TV and help it reach more people. And if you want Bob to be your circuit rider, then give me the strength and wisdom to carry it through, for Christ's sake, amen."

I am writing this one month after that night. Bob's January *Heartbeat* will be in the mail next week, announcing, "Bob, The Circuit Rider." He has secured the bus: a used Continental Trailway Bus. It has a study room, bunks for eight, and a bathroom. It has plenty of space for all the books, records and equipment.

I should say he has tentatively done this, because he is counting heavily on people helping him secure a down-payment on the bus. I would bet they will.

He has secured a fine man, Max Carter, who was a bus driver for five years. Max is already handling the books and records. He will also be bus driver, probably by the time this book reaches the public.

He has already begun re-shuffling his schedule. I know this could upset some, but I hope it won't. There will be enough factors working against this venture. I hope the one thing Bob will be able to count on will be the prayers and support of fellow Christians.

You may feel this whole idea is rather brazen, or sensational, or impulsive. And you may be correct in all your feelings.

But what if you were a preacher? And what if you were convinced that God had laid America on your heart and given you the seventies to reach your nation for Him?

And what if you found yourself dreaming at night that it was up to you to see that, in America, every eye saw, and every ear heard, and every heart felt that it was fun being saved?

And what if you had done your best in 1973—accomplishing more than the previous 14 years combined—and found you had not yet begun to reach all America?

And what if a friend of yours, who was already on more TV stations than any man alive, were to say to you, "Here's an idea that will help you cover America," what would you do?

Bob bought a bus.

Bob signing autographs for his favorite fans.

CHAPTER XII

Will the Real Bob Harrington Please Stand Up? AN EVALUATION

The preceding pages have presented a year in the life of a minister; not an average minister, nor an average year, even for him. It, of course, will be left to the reader to determine what to make of these experiences. Surely, what some may call courage, others may call foolheartedness. Is Bob Harrington a hero, a villain, or a fool?

How does one qualify for the role of hero? Hopefully it does not come from unanimous consent, for there are some persons for whom Bob Harrington will never be a hero.

Such a person wrote Bob the following letter this past year. The person's name will be withheld since permission has not been requested for its use.

Dear Mr. Harrington

Here is the book I wanted you to read concerning Biblical Evangelism. I have listened to most of your

recorded messages, and I can't find much of the glory
and the grace of Jesus Christ in them. There is far too
much "Bob" and not enough of the Word of God. Sinners may laugh at your clever anecdotes and illustra-
tions and may become emotionally stirred up, but
where is the awakening of sinners to see their lost,
hopeless, helpless, dead condition outside of Christ?

May I be brutally frank? Your message and your
methods have little in common with the Gospel of God
as proclaimed by the Apostles of the Lord. If you are
preaching a half-gospel, then Galatians 1:8-9 will apply
to you also. I will be praying for you.

Sincerely in Christ (name withheld)

How does one qualify for the role of hero? The answer
is simple. There must be one person who thinks of him as
his hero; not two, or two hundred, or two thousand. For
one is the only qualitative number that exists, in that it
defines the quality, or essence, of a given property. The
difference between two and two million is strictly quanti-
tative. But the difference between zero and one is infi-
nite.

So we must, to qualify Bob Harrington, find one person
for whom Bob is a hero. I submit, for your consideration,
Gary Lee Piecznski. He was one among thousands when
Bob first passed his way. He became unique and distinct
when Bob received the following letter from his mother.

Dear Brother Bob

This letter will be about our young son, Gary Lee
Piecznski, who went to live with the Lord, December
8, 1972 at the age of sixteen years old.

Gary used to write you real often requesting litera-
ture, records, books and materials you offered on your
weekly TV shows. He had just received the lapel pin
3 days before he died and the very day he became ill.
He was buried with the lapel pin as it was the first and
only time he was to wear it.

Our family first became aware of you through your
visit to Houston, Spring of 1972. I saw you on the
Dialing For Dollars show and the Steve Edwards show.
You said you would be at Woodridge Baptist Church
that weekend. We missed the first night but were able
to make it Saturday night, both services Sunday morning and Sunday night. Our sons, as we, were so impressed by you. Our four sons and I were able to sit on
the second row from the front on that Sunday morning. We are of the Methodist Faith, and are members
of St. Andrew's United Methodist Church. We had
decided to stay during both the Sunday School and
Church hours. You autographed the boys' Bibles. One
is 18, Gary was 16, Cary is 12, and Rodney is 4 years.
The one 18 is Larry and by the way he has become a
Baptist and we are real proud of him for making his
own decision. It was the Lord's will.

We took Gary as well as other members of our
family to see you at Woodridge Baptist Church this
past October 1972 when you were there. Gary was the
only one from our family who got up and had the
calling on Friday night, October 6th to rededicate his
life to our Lord and Saviour two months before he
died. Gary was saved in 1969. He never gave us a specific date. Before he left the service that night, he spent
his own $5 to buy the book, "Eight Days With Bob
Harrington" which he was still reading and marked at
the time of his death. You autographed it for him. He
was as proud of your signature as he was of his Bible
you had signed in the Spring. . . . Gary became ill on
Wednesday, December 6, 1972. He was admitted to
the hospital for the last time and Gary knew it. He

told us on Thursday, the day he was admitted, that he would die soon and that he would be living with the Lord. He was happy but that he hated to do this to us right at Christmas time. The London type flu went into double pneumonia real fast. He passed away at 10:40 P.M. Friday, December 8th, 1972. Gary was truly saved and had been saved for four years.

Bob Harrington, you were Gary's real hero. Every boy has a hero and you were his. He signed all his papers "It's Fun Being Saved." He also put the year. I am enclosing one of his papers for you to see it.

. . . God bless you for influencing our son's life. He loved you.

Yours in Christ

Mrs. D. L. Piecznski

P.S. We are considering having "It's Fun Being Saved" on the Piecznski monument instead of a Scripture verse.

Garey Precznke

Its fun being saved

year 67

Virgiana	X		New Indiana	✓
Tennessee	✓		Kansas	
South Caloruna	X		Kenucky	X
Pennsyvania	✓		Louisiana	✓
New Hampshier	X ✓		Missouri	✓✓
Massauce			Mississippi	✓
Maine	✓		Nebraska	✓✓
Iowa	✓		Minnisota	✓
Illinois			Nevada	✓
Albamba	X		Michigan	
Alaska	✓		Oregon	
Arizona	✓		New Jersey	✓
Arkansas	✓		Ohloma	X
California	✓		New Mexico	✓✓
Colarda	X		Ohio	✓✓
Connectic	X		Washington	✓✓
Delware	✓		Utah	✓✓
Florida	✓		Wyoming	✓✓
Georgia	✓		West Virgina	
Hawaii	✓			
Odio	X